BRIGHT NOTES

1984
BY
GEORGE ORWELL

Intelligent Education

Nashville, Tennessee

BRIGHT NOTES: 1984
www.BrightNotes.com

No part of this publication may be used or reproduced in any manner whatsoever without written permission, except in the case of brief quotations in critical articles and reviews. For permissions, contact Influence Publishers http://www.influencepublishers.com.

ISBN: 978-1-645421-68-9 (Paperback)
ISBN: 978-1-645421-69-6 (eBook)

Published in accordance with the U.S. Copyright Office Orphan Works and Mass Digitization report of the register of copyrights, June 2015.

Originally published by Monarch Press.
Ralph A. Ranald, 1965
2020 Edition published by Influence Publishers.

Interior design by Lapiz Digital Services. Cover Design by Thinkpen Designs.

Printed in the United States of America.

Library of Congress Cataloging-in-Publication Data forthcoming.
Names: Intelligent Education
Title: BRIGHT NOTES: 1984
Subject: STU004000 STUDY AIDS / Book Notes

CONTENTS

1)	Introduction to George Orwell	1
2)	An Introduction to 1984: Structure and Meaning	17
3)	Textual Analysis	
	Part One, Sections 1–3	36
	Part One, Sections 4–8	55
	Part Two	73
	Part Three	89
4)	Appendix	100
5)	Character Analyses	105
6)	Critical Commentary	113
7)	Essay Questions and Answers	125

GEORGE ORWELL

INTRODUCTION

In 1943, the year of Europe's greatest self-destruction and for Western civilization possibly the most hopeless year of this century, George Orwell published an essay called "Looking Back on the Spanish War." In that essay, there appears a poem dedicated to an anonymous soldier of the war, a war (1936-39) in which Orwell himself served as a volunteer. Orwell had seen the soldier who was the subject of his poem, and whose name he never did learn, in 1936 soon after he had come to Spain to be a soldier in the revolutionary militia.

The poem is not a great one; Orwell was not primarily a poet. But the last **stanza** is of some significance for a consideration of the man George Orwell as well as his work. Orwell addresses this unknown soldier, who stands for all ordinary soldiers who fought in this destructive Civil War in Spain:

But the thing that I saw in your face No power can disinherit:
No bomb that ever burst, Shatters the crystal spirit.

"No bomb that ever burst, shatters the crystal spirit." The line is typical of Orwell. It could stand as an epigraph or slogan, though he himself was skeptical of slogans, for George Orwell's own life and what he stood for, or thought he stood for: the dignity of man, the inviolability of the human spirit, and each man's right to spiritual privacy. Man has, in the language of the American Declaration of Independence, "certain inalienable rights," and it is the inalienability of these rights which Orwell affirmed in all his works, whether they are novels, as is *1984,* or political satires, such as *Animal Farm,* or individual essays on literary, political, and social matters, or books such as *Burmese Days* or *Homage to Catalonia,* which might best be called "political autobiographies." Consequently, it is something of a paradox that Orwell's deservedly great reputation today rests primarily on *1984,* a work which seems to contain the deepest pessimism about man's nature. But the two views of Orwell, as a pessimist about man's capacity for the total enslavement of his fellows, and as an optimist and affirmer of the human spirit, can be reconciled by study of his biography and of the body of his writings, especially as they bear on that biography.

1984 is a dark work, at least on the surface, and there seems little of affirmation about it. It has given words and phrases to the English language: Thoughtcrime, Newspeak, Big Brother, the Two Minutes' Hate, the Proles, the Thought Police. But these, all of which are concepts characterizing the nightmare world of *1984*, require further explanation than that provided in the novel and that explanation may be found in large measure in the biography of George Orwell. While works such as *1984* and *Down and Out in Paris and London* may stand alone and be read without reference to biographical material, a consideration of that material casts additional light on their meaning. It is to that biography that we now turn.

Orwell was born Eric Hugh Blair in 1903 in Motihari, Bengal, an area in eastern India only about three hundred miles from

Burma, where Orwell was to serve twenty years later as a British civil servant. He was the only son of a subordinate British civil servant; his father, serving in the British Raj (government) of India, worked in the Customs and Excise department the government. Apparently Orwell's father was reserved and distant with his children. Orwell had a sister about five years old than he, and another five years younger, but he was never very close to his sisters either. Indeed, by his own account his attitude toward his immediate family was largely negative (except for his relationship with his mother). This attitude is revealed in what Orwell said about his early childhood in his famous essay "Such, Such Were the Joys..." which deals with his unhappy career at an English preparatory school. As a salaried official without an independent income, Orwell's father does not seem to have been well off financially. This poverty was to haunt our novelist, causing him to dwell almost obsessively on matters of social class and social distinction. Indeed, Orwell was on one occasion to describe the social class into which he was born as "lower upper-middle," perhaps with a touch of **irony** at such attempts at precise classification.

In 1911, at a very early age, Orwell was sent back to England to begin his education. These were the last quiet years of the pre-World War I era, when the imperial power of England was unquestioned and when it was necessary to have a constant supply of young men who, learning the art and science of ruling in England, would come out to India, Burma, and other far reaches of the British Empire to staff the government offices. And such a career - his father's - seems at this point to have been Orwell's destiny. Thus, the lengthy enforced separation from his family - there was certainly not enough money for the boy to make visits back to India - followed a quite usual pattern among the English upper and middle classes. The educational system which was based on a rather rigid class structure had narrow but clearly defined goals based on a philosophy of education which had been developing in England at least since the sixteenth century. This system was to have a profound effect on George Orwell, much of whose writing was to become either a commentary on or a criticism of it.

The preparatory school he attended beginning at age eight was located on the southern coast of England; it is the school to which he referred, though not by its actual name, in the essay "Such, Such Were the Joys…" This essay is a biting, indeed a bitter attack on the kind of education which was respected among certain social classes in Great Britain; and although Orwell disguised the name of the school by calling it "Crossgates" the essay has still never been legally published in England because of the possibility of a libel suit involving the good name of the school. Orwell was to be a boarding student at the school for five years, from 1911 through 1916.

Orwell's parents seem to have been less well-to-do than the parents of most of the other students at "Crossgates." Orwell relates in his essay that by indirect means he gradually came to realize that Mr. and Mrs. Simpson, the Headmaster and Headmistress of the school (nicknamed by the boys respectively Sim and Bingo) had taken on young George, or Eric, as he was then called, as a sort of investment, at reduced tuition and boarding fees. However, as he saw the case, they did this not out of concern for his welfare, but rather because they thought he was bright and expected that with proper instruction he would win valuable scholarships to some of the great public schools, such as Eton, Winchester, or Wellington. This achievement would in turn help to add luster to the school's name and, as it was a private institution run in some measure for profit, attract more and wealthier students to it. The boy did not disappoint them in this respect, because he won scholarships both to Eton, which he ultimately attended and which is one of the most famous as well as one of the oldest public schools in England, and to Wellington.

But there were a number of things about the preparatory school which he detested, and which, from his own account, were to scar him psychologically. Thus, even the title of his essay is a bitterly ironic one. In his *Songs of Innocence,* the eighteenth-century poet William Blake has a poem called "The Ecchoing Green," the middle **stanza** of which paints a picture of the idealized innocence and joyfulness of childhood:

Old John, with white hair, Does laugh away care, Sitting under the oak, Among the old folk. They laugh at our play, And soon they all say: "Such, such were the joys When we all, girls and boys, In our youth time were seen On the Ecchoing Green."

But for the young Eric Blair, there were to be no idyllic times at Crossgates. He was rudely awakened by the stern regimen of the school. Beatings were commonplace. He recounts in the essay that soon after he arrived, at age eight, he was beaten by the Headmaster, Sim, for wetting his bed. He initially made light of the beating, though it was with a bone-handled riding crop; however, Sim overheard him tell his fellow students outside the room that "It didn't hurt," and he was immediately beaten again. This time the Headmaster used such force that he broke the handle of the riding crop while beating him to the point where he collapsed "into a chair, weakly snivelling."

This beating marked the start of an educational process which was to instill in the young Eric Blair an awful conviction of worthlessness, guilt, and weakness, which by his own account, he was not able to overcome for years. "This was," he wrote in "Such, Such Were the Joys . . .," "the great abiding lesson of my boyhood: that I was in a world where it was not possible for me to be good . . . it brought home to me for the first time the harshness of the environment into which I had been flung." He did not add, though he might have, that the real or fancied maltreatment at Crossgates was not only to scar him psychologically, but to develop in him certain characteristic interests, to intensify his preoccupation with certain themes, such as the effect of prolonged punishment on the human spirit, the relative importance of heredity and environment, the possibility of brainwashing (especially important in *1984*), and the oppression, as he saw it, so often visited on the defenseless, whether they were the poor of India or Burma, or the unassertive English boarding-school student such as he fancied himself to be at this time. At Crossgates, the boy was beaten for being a chronic bed-wetter - something which he literally could not help - and underwent the usual "fagging" [hazing] at the hands of the older boys. What he especially resented was the favoritism which he believed he saw in the treatment meted out by the Headmaster: the boys whose parents were wealthy and titled were treated with much more consideration than were the poorer boys who were attending the school at reduced tuition rates.

The formal curriculum had the classical bias usual at such a school; the students started Latin at age eight, Greek at age ten. But much of the learning in the classical languages was to Eric Blair the dullest kind of rote learning. He was, as a scholarship student, being prepared to take a competitive examination at age twelve or thirteen - an examination which would determine his entire future. For if he was successful in it, he would win a scholarship to a public school; if he failed, he would undoubtedly become, as the Headmaster frequently told him, "a little office boy at forty pounds a year." The studies emphasized anything which might contribute to his passing the examination, but he felt that while the system may have been efficient in that it achieved its objective, it could not truly be called education.

Though Bingo and Sim frequently reminded him of how much they had done for him, a scholarship boy who was "living on their bounty," he was not grateful. Instead, he said in "Such, Such Were the Joys..." "I hated both of them. I could not control my subjective feelings, and I could not control them from myself." This point in Orwell's biography may be important for the light it casts on the ambivalent way in which Winston Smith, the oppressed little man representative of much in his society in *1984*, regards Big Brother, For the young Eric Blair, the authorities of his preparatory school, especially Sim and Bingo, stood in the same relationship to him as did Big Brother to Winston Smith; indeed the latter situation may well have been suggested by the former. The lack of privacy in the living quarters of the school, the oppression with the encouragement of Sim and Bingo, of the weaker boys by the stronger, the spying, especially in search of heterodox behavior or sexual misdemeanors among the boys, the "squalor and neglect... the W. C. [water closet, or lavatory] and dirty-handkerchief side of life," as Orwell called it-all these were to appear in his writing, though changed and magnified. The worst thing about Crossgates, then, in Orwell's view was that it violated his integrity, and attempted to deny to him the sole possession of that corner of his mind or consciousness which was, or should have been, forever and inalienably his. This **theme**, too, of the ultimate blasphemy of the violation of sovereign personality, reappears in *1984*.

In fairness to the proprietors of Crossgates, it must be said that Orwell's view of the school and the influence it was to have on his life and thought was highly subjective (as he himself stated in his essay about this period of his life.) Christopher Hollis, a friend and contemporary of George Orwell at Eton and the author of a biographical-critical study of him refers to the Crossgates **episode** in more balanced terms, as though the school was not objectively quite as bad as Orwell painted it - though some of the abuses which Orwell mentioned no doubt did in fact exist. But the important point is not the objective reality of the school, but the effect which it had on Orwell during a key phase in his development. He had a sense of inferiority and failure which haunted him. In a world made for the strong, he was convinced that he was doomed not to succeed, because in any case, in the terms of the rigid social code drummed into him at Crossgates, "success was measured not by what you did but by what you were." Even after he had won his two excellent scholarships, to Eton and to Wellington, he felt that Sim and Bingo and the school rejected him. He was not in good health, having defective bronchial tubes and a minor lesion on one lung which, it may be, helped to occasion his untimely death at age forty-seven. But beyond any physical deficiencies, real or imagined, was the awful sense of failure and of the bonds of class and birth. "In a world where the prime necessities were money, titled relatives, athleticism, tailor-made clothes, neatly brushed hair, a charming smile, I was no good." Such were his words about himself at the time he left Crossgates forever.

By his proficiency at Crossgates in the study of Latin and Greek, under the urgings (and beatings) of Sim and Bingo, Orwell won a scholarship which would maintain him at Eton for a complete education, provided his scholastic performance was satisfactory. Thus, in 1917, when Orwell was fourteen years old, he matriculated at Eton. In the public schools the students were given much more freedom to manage their own affairs that was the case at the preparatory schools, and as Orwell himself said in "Such, Such Were the Joys . . .," he became an idler where his studies were concerned. After the years of cramming in Latin and Greek, he did only enough at Eton to maintain a class standing that would permit him to retain his scholarship, and no more. But he read widely, and even at this point in his life he impressed those around him as being an intellectual. To Cyril Connolly one of his acquaintances at Eton, he proved by the force of his example "that there existed an alternative to character, Intelligence." His reading included Shaw, Samuel Butler, and others who might be described as the great questioners of Victorian life, and whose practice reinforced Orwell's own tendency to ask embarrassing questions about society.

While Orwell said that he was not well liked by the other boys at Eton, in part because of his poverty, this does not seem to be true. Christopher Hollis, two years ahead of him at Eton and therefore roughly his contemporary in the school, says that Orwell was regarded as something of a leader of the other boys, and also that in an environment in which beatings were a part of the system, he was in fact beaten rather less than the others. But Orwell's final judgment on Eton, published in an article in the Observer, "For Ever Eton," on August 1, 1948, described the school as offering "a tolerant and civilized atmosphere which gives each boy a fair chance of developing his individuality."

Orwell graduated from Eton at age eighteen, and rather unexpectedly, was to spend the next five years (1922-27) in Burma as an officer of the Indian Imperial Police. For a young man graduating from a public school like Eton, the normal next step would have been entrance to Oxford or Cambridge for three years of further study and a University degree. And apparently Orwell could have had this, for Eton provided scholarships for some of its students who might not otherwise have had the opportunity to attend a University. Though the circumstances are somewhat obscure, Orwell, according to Christopher Hollis, was persuaded by one of his teachers at Eton that he ought to bypass the University route. "You've had enough of education.

Take a job abroad and see something of the world," his teacher allegedly told him, and though Orwell was rather to regret this decision later, he entered the service of the British Government as a civil servant in Burma.

He apparently was a good officer, for he did have the habit of command. But he became increasingly disillusioned with his job, and ceased to believe in the beneficial effects of imperialism, even British imperialism. He felt that all Europeans, as he said in his essay "Marrakech," are essentially fooling the peoples under colonial domination, and he developed, during his five years in the British service, a tremendous amount of guilt at his supposedly privileged position. This guilt feeling simply reinforced the feeling of general "worthlessness" which had been built up during his preparatory school years. His experience in Burma is perhaps best illustrated in the famous essay "Shooting an Elephant," written a number of years after the fact, in which his performance of his duty as a police officer in Moulmein, Lower Burma, becomes the occasion for a graphic comment on what he saw as the essential self-imprisonment of all who served the cause of the British Government in its imperial domains.

Feeling stifled, therefore, by his job Orwell came home on leave in 1927 and never returned to Burma, instead resigning from the service. The Burmese experience was very valuable to him is his formation as an artist and a thinker, but torture to him as a man because of his sensitivity to what he thought of as the shortcomings of imperialism. Out of his Burmese experience was to come his first novel, *Burmese Days,* published in 1934, seven years after his return from Burma. As is the case in every Orwell novel, there is one character in *Burmese Days* who has many of the qualities of Orwell himself, and with whom Orwell consciously or unconsciously identified. That character is named Flory-also a civil servant in the British Raj in Burma who deteriorates under the influence of the system. But Orwell himself, fearing that the system would ruin him both ethically and emotionally if he remained a part of it, left the service, while Flory stayed in it until it indirectly at least brought about his death.

From 1927 until 1933 Orwell led what must have been an unprecedented life for a young man of his ability and education. Explanations of his motivation for leading this life are still vague; perhaps the truth will never be known. But out of these years of great poverty and deprivation came, in 1933, his first book, *Down and Out in Paris and London*, a most graphic and subjective study of poverty and its effect upon the human spirit, and certainly one of the most truthful books on the subject that has ever been written.

Orwell at this time changed his name from Eric Blair. "George" is a traditional English name, the patron Saint of England being St. George, who is known for fighting with dragons, as Orwell metaphorically fought with himself and the world. "Orwell" is the name of a small river in Suffolk, by which he once lived; the symbolism of this name may involve simply his returning to the land, the earth, out of the rarefied background of an Etonian education. But his reasons are really obscure. It appears that he had such a strong feeling of guilt over the class privilege from which he had benefited, first at Eton and then in Burma, that he rejected this privilege and turned his back on his social class by changing his name and living in poverty for nearly six years. The concern with the sheer physical side of poverty and deprivation which we find in *1984* stems from this period in Orwell's life.

After his return from the lower depths of poverty in 1933, a year which, significantly, coincided with the rise to power of Hitler in Germany, Orwell averaged about a book a year until World War

II and his declining health made this rate of literary production impossible. Poverty, whether lower-class or, something which he personally regarded as worse, lower middle-class, was his subject in his next two novels, *A Clergyman's Daughter* (1935), and *Keep the Aspidistra Flying* (1936).

The first is a book about the impoverishment, physical and spiritual, of moneyless middle-class genteel life in an English vicarage and in a dreadful and cheap girls' private school. The second is an even more powerful work about a conflict between Bohemianism and normal middle-class respectability which at least affirms the continuance of life; the hero, Gordon Comstock, strongly resembles Orwell himself. Both novels cast some light on Orwell's preoccupations in his masterpiece, *1984,* with those pressures which erode the human spirit. Two of the worst of these are poverty and deprivation, tools which the Party in *1984* uses because it desires the degradation of man.

By 1936, he was earning enough from writing - no small trick in an England still undergoing the depression - to live in the country away from London. In 1936 he began a survey of unemployment in England and its effects. This resulted in 1937 in *The Road to Wigan Pier*, which the Left Book Club, which commissioned it, was to print while at the same time disclaiming responsibility for the views Orwell expressed in it. In this book he spoke of socialism as a possible remedy for the conditions which he so excellently described out of firsthand knowledge and emotional understanding.

He married Eileen O'Shaughnessy in 1936, and the marriage seems to have been a happy one, even an ideal relationship. Leaving the manuscript of *The Road to Wigan Pier* with those who had commissioned it, before they could argue with him over its content, Orwell and his wife went to Spain, where the Spanish

Civil War had broken out in that year. Orwell wished to study the Civil War and had received a publisher's advance to write a book about it. Quite characteristically, he decided that the best way to study the war was to fight in it. He became a member of the P. O. U. M. (Partido Obrero de Unificacion Marxista, translated as Workers' Party of Marxist Unification). This was a radical Socialist-Trotskyite militia force which was opposed to the Communist-Stalinists of the International Brigades. As it turned out, the two factions ended up fighting each other as bitterly as they were to fight the Fascist forces of General Francisco Franco. The P. O. U. M. was ruthlessly suppressed by Stalin's agents and their collaborators, and many Spanish members who had joined the P. O. U. M. wishing only to fight those who had rebelled against the Republican Government of Spain were arrested and executed. Orwell was badly wounded in the throat in fighting on the front lines, and then was under such suspicion as a member of the P. O. U. M. that he and his wife were lucky to escape from Spain with their lives. It is probable that his being a British subject helped him to escape, but others among his friends were not so lucky, and were killed or died in prison. This experience acquainted him at firsthand with the nature of totalitarianism, for Spain, from 1936 to 1939, may be described, though the terms are over-simplified, as a battleground between the two chief forms of totalitarian regime of our century, fascism and communism. Out of this period came Orwell's book about his experience in Spain, *Homage to Catalonia* (1938). Orwell regarded the actions of the Communists in Spain as a betrayal of the popular revolution which might otherwise have given the working classes real freedom and status. This idea is to spill over into the presentation of the Party in *1984* and the divergence between its theory and its practice.

1939 saw the publication of *Coming Up for Air,* a combination of nostalgia for pre-World War I times and conservative England,

and apprehension at the appearance of "the streamlined men from Eastern Europe, who thought in slogans and spoke in bullets." After 1939, with the outbreak of World War II, Orwell devoted himself to writing on behalf of the war effort and to service as a sergeant in the Home Guard in England (he was rejected for military service because of his impaired health). He broadcast and wrote for the B. B. C., and also wrote many essays, containing qualified but sincere praise of English institutions and ways when compared with the ways of the totalitarian regimes of Hitler, Mussolini, and Stalin. As a result of his Spanish experience, Orwell was less deceived than most about Stalin's objectives in allowing Russia's entry into the war in 1941. And even in the fever of war hysteria, when England was fighting for its very existence, Orwell spoke out for reason and for the facing of cold facts, whether about the Germans or about those who were less frank in their devotion to dictatorial forms of government. All totalitarianism was wrong, in Orwell's view, as it involved a denial of the basic dignity of man. Thus *The Lion and the Unicorn*, published in 1941, was a pamphlet containing three essays: "Shopkeepers at War," "The English Revolution," and "England, Your England." The last of these is the most famous, but all three describe what Orwell thinks of the English people. On a comparative basis, he says, they at least are more devoted than most to the principles of decency and human freedom which make life worth living.

Animal Farm, which with *1984* would make Orwell world famous, was written between November, 1943, and February, 1944. For sometime Orwell was unable to find a publisher for it. This was due in part to the wartime condition of paper scarcity, but also to the fact that Russia was an ally and it was perceived that *Animal Farm* was a **satire** on the rise of totalitarian government in Russia under Lenin, Trotsky, and Stalin. It is political satire — especially reminiscent of Book IV of *Gulliver's Travels* — perhaps the best English satire on communism. Its genesis was really in Orwell's experience in Spain, as has been pointed out, and when *Animal Farm* finally appeared in August, 1945, it was at that point where the Western Allies were becoming disenchanted with the Stalin regime and the possibilities of cooperating with it in the construction of a viable postwar order. Thus, the hour and the book were exactly matched, and the inevitable result was that Orwell's book, being widely translated, became world famous.

In this year, 1945, Orwell's wife died as the result of a minor operation. He attributed her death to lowered physical resistance due to the war; both she and Orwell had consistently given up a part of their wartime food rations to feed children, and consequently had impaired their health. But this was in keeping with their character; both have been described by friends as having something of the saintly ascetic in their makeups.

1984 came out of the chaotic postwar period, 1945-49, and was written in the state of depression and pessimism occasioned by the unexpected death of Orwell's wife and by his own poor health. In this period he learned that he was suffering from tuberculosis, and that he would have to rest if his life were to be saved. Instead, out of a sense of duty and an overwhelming urge to express what he had learned of totalitarianism, he wrote *1984*. Off the coast of western Scotland, about a hundred miles west of Glasgow, there is an island off the beaten track: the island of Jura. There, in 1947, Orwell went with the infant son whom he and his wife had adopted, taking along his sister to act as the nurse, and there he worked to finish *1984*. In January, 1949, *1984* was finished, and his friend Richard Rees accompanied him from Jura to a sanitarium in Gloucestershire.

Orwell's health was shattered. He had a few months of happiness in 1949 when in the early summer he married Sonia

Brownell, who assisted him in taking care of his adopted son. On January 21, 1950, as he was about to leave for a sanitarium in Switzerland, he had a tubercular hemmorhage and died. While it is clear that the condition of his health in his last years had something to do with the thoughts he expressed in *1984,* and the personal tragedies he underwent also contributed to this end, it must be remembered that essentially all of his life and work was a preparation for writing *1984;* this is one of the reasons for studying his biography and his other novels and essays carefully quite apart from their intrinsic interest. He was writing in *1984* about what he had once called "the central question . . . how to prevent power from being abused." *Animal Farm* was a study and a history of this subject from a different point of view and in a different literary **genre** - the beast fable rather than (as in *1984*) the anti-Utopia. But his abiding preoccupation was with the reconcilement of human liberty and the affirmation of the human spirit with the exercise of power which must of necessity exist if society is to exist. Behind this preoccupation was his belief in the human race and in the necessity of its survival in freedom.

1984

AN INTRODUCTION: STRUCTURE AND MEANING

The novel, it should be said at the outset of this discussion, is not presented by Orwell as an objective prediction of what life in the year 1984 will be like. It would be more accurate to describe it as a projection of certain tendencies, an exaggerated picture as seen in a series of distorted mirrors of what life in the future might be like if what Orwell saw as the logical outcome of these present tendencies were to come to pass. His purpose in writing this great satirical work of political fiction was, we can deduce from the total pattern of his life and his writings, to ensure, as far as it lay in his power, that the kind of society which he envisioned in *1984* would never come about. *1984,* then, is a **satire** whose purpose is not to portray the future, but to warn the present: to place those whom Orwell considered the decent members of his own generation on guard. And his definition of the decent people was quite simple: it appears in its least complicated form, as we shall see, in a novel of Orwell's much less well known than *1984*: *Coming Up for Air*. In the world, as Orwell saw it developing, fear, hatred, sadism, and insane glorification of brute force are in the ascendancy. As George Bowling, the forty-five year old hero of *Coming Up for*

Air, thinks of the coming European war (1939) which is sure to tear everything to pieces, he says: "Every thinking person nowadays is stiff with fright." In turn, the omnipresent fear leads to violence - "smashing people's faces in with a spanner [wrench]." At a climactic moment in *1984,* O'Brien, who is Winston Smith's torturer and Grand Inquisitor in the cellars of the Thought Police, says to him: "If you want a picture of the future, imagine a boot stamping on a human face-forever." It is this picture to which all decent people, all those who are not disposed to go around smashing people's faces in with spanners or with anything else, should be opposed. It was what Orwell opposed in his life and his writings, almost literally until his last breath. *1984,* then, was written in this spirit: to help recall men once again, in what Orwell saw as a completely secularized age, to a sense of decency and of the dignity of man.

Orwell, then, in *1984* was writing political **satire** of an activist nature because he hoped that his work might have some political effect by alerting its readers to certain dangers which he saw. It is in the tradition of Utopian literature which, taking its name from Sir Thomas More's *Utopia* (written 1515-16) but extending back at least to Plato's *Republic,* describes a mythical but ideal society which is intended to cast light on society as it actually is and to change the reality to conform more to the author's view of the ideal. A variant of Utopian literature is the "anti-Utopia," in which the mythical or hypothetical is presented not as an ideal, but as a distortion and exaggeration of the real, often emphasizing the worst and most disagreeable tendencies of real society. Its objective is the same as that of the true Utopia, that is, men are urged to improve the society in which they live, but instead of presenting an ideal society or state of being which men might consider as a model of the more perfect society which the author of Utopian literature would like to see come about, the author of an anti-Utopia presents a satirical criticism of mankind's pride and folly, coupled with a warning that if the tendencies illustrated in the anti-Utopia are not checked, the condition of man will inevitably get worse instead of better. The most famous anti-Utopian satirical fiction in English is *Gulliver's Travels* (1726). But despite the existence of such other works in this tradition as Aldous Huxley's *Brave New World* (1932), Orwell's *1984* is without doubt the most famous and influential anti-Utopian work of the twentieth century.

The true structure of the grim society of *1984* is explained in a synthetic political tract which Orwell includes in the book and which Winston Smith reads as he is about to be captured by the Thought Police; this tract is called *The Theory and Practice of Oligarchical Collectivism*, by Emmanuel Goldstein, who is the archenemy of Big Brother, the Leader, and of the Party which controls the society of *1984*. Oligarchy is that form of government in which a small group exercises control (the word is not used as a compliment, as there is a suggestion in it that such a form is corrupt). Certainly the oligarchical society of *1984* is corrupt; in fact, it exists because the small group which rules it maintains itself by tyrannizing and corrupting the large majority of the people.

The society of *1984* in Oceania, one of the three superstates into which the world is divided, has three classes: the Inner Party, the Outer Party, and the Proles. The Inner Party numbers only two per cent of the population; it is the ruling class, maintaining its numbers not by hereditary succession, democratic election, or brute force, but rather by selection of small numbers from time to time either from children of Inner Party members or from the most able members of the Outer Party. It is a selective aristocracy of talent — talent of a kind appropriate to such a society, and including both intelligence and vigorous devotion to the aims of the Party. Big Brother, whose pictures and statues are everywhere in *1984,* is the symbol of the Inner Party: the Leader of the State. It is never clear whether he has an objective existence as a person, but most likely he does not: he is simply the imaginary representative of the power elite of the Inner Party, and has been created by the Inner Party out of a perception that men have a psychological necessity for a single all-powerful leader. The only member of the Inner Party whom we ever meet in the book in any detail is O'Brien, the torturer of Winston Smith; significantly, we never learn O'Brien's first name, and indeed only three characters in the depersonalized and dehumanized world of *1984* are ever given their complete names in this novel.

Under the complete control of the Inner Party is the Outer Party, composing fifteen per cent of the population of *1984* in Oceania. It does the dirty work: all of the routine administration is handled by the Outer Party, which may be described as a relatively small, powerless, but indispensable middle class. A few of its most ambitious and intelligent members, who might cause trouble if they were held permanently in subservient positions, are made harmless to the State by allowing them to rise into the Inner Party.

Winston Smith, the thirty-nine-year-old hero of *1984,* is a member of the Outer Party. The plot of the book revolves around Winston's revolt against his strait-jacket society, and the end to which that revolt leads him. Even the complete name of our hero is of symbolic significance: coupled to his last name, Smith, which is the most common name in English-speaking lands and which gives a suggestion that Smith is representative man, or Everyman, is the name, Winston, which is the first name of the great war leader and Prime Minister who is generally recognized as the greatest Englishman of his age, Winston Churchill. Winston Smith, then, in the terms of *1984* is Everyman, and at the same time he is quite unique. For at the beginning of the book, Winston Smith, a minor employee of the Government's Ministry of Truth, sets his will against Big Brother and the Party, even though he realizes that such disobedience can have only one end. All crimes in *1984* are comprehended in one master crime: Thoughtcrime, which consists in having an improper mental or inner attitude with respect to the Party and to Big Brother, and though this crime is not even denounced in any written law, everyone knows what it is and also knows that it is punishable by death with or without a formal legal trial. Winston is a Thoughtcriminal, and the book, in illustrating his decline and fall, takes the reader on a tour of the most representative parts of the entire society so that he many understand its structure as well as its past history.

The government in *1984* is monolithic and centralized. In London, capital city of Airstrip One (England), a province of Oceania, the government of which Winston Smith is a minor employee is organized in four gigantic Ministries: the Ministry of Truth, which is involved with news, entertainment, education, and the fine arts; the Ministry of Peace, which concerns itself with war; the Ministry of Love, which maintains law and order and which administers the secret police; and the Ministry of Plenty, which is responsible for economic affairs. In Newspeak, the official, abbreviated language of *1984,* these are called respectively Minitrue, Minipax, Miniluv, and Miniplenty. Winston Smith is an employee of the Ministry of Truth.

As we first meet Winston Smith, he is at work in the Ministry of Truth. His job is to rewrite (really to falsify) history to conform to Party doctrine, in keeping with the Party slogan, which will be more fully discussed hereafter: "Who controls the Past controls the Future." At the point of our first acquaintance with our hero, Winston has, on April 4, 1984, begun to keep a diary.

This is not technically illegal, for nothing in *1984* is illegal since there are no written laws, but it is dangerous nevertheless; it shows that one may harbor private thoughts and by committing them to paper may wish in some way to communicate these thoughts to other persons. And part of the maintenance of the oligarchical totalitarian form of government in *1984* depends not on increasing communication, but on decreasing it to the minimum necessary to carry on the routine of life. Therefore Winston's act is suspect, and he knows it.

The three slogans of the Party, upon which the theory of government in *1984* ultimately rests, are:

War Is Peace Freedom Is Slavery Ignorance Is Strength

These three slogans are explained to Winston as he reads Emmanuel Goldstein's book, *The Theory and Practice of Oligarchical Collectivism*. What they mean will be considered in the analytic portions of the present study, but at this time the first - "War Is Peace" - should be explained briefly. For the state of society in *1984* in all three superstates is the same. Eurasia, Eastasia, and Oceania are all self-contained economies having little or no need of external support. They have sufficient raw materials within their boundaries so that additional supplies are not essential. At most, war can provide them with a few additional millions of people for hard labor, and a relatively few square miles of minimally useful land. Yet, despite the fact that war is in no way an economic necessity, the rulers of all three superstates see to it that a constant state of war is maintained. Society is organized on a war footing. Except for the highly favored two per cent of the population who are the decision-makers (the Inner Party), the people (the Outer Party and the Proles) live in conditions of overcrowding, chronic shortage of food and all other goods, bad plumbing, shoddy materials and workmanship, and long hours of work at low pay, with added "voluntary" work for Outer Party members (work offered as a gesture of loyalty to the State and to Big Brother, for which no pay is received).

But in the past, war had an objective which, according to Goldstein's analysis of past societies, was largely economic. In *1984,* on the other hand, the purpose of war is not to win- definitely not to win -but instead to maintain the status quo. War, therefore, is indeed Peace, because the state of perpetual war keeps society in balance. War is Peace for as long as the war exists but does not become too "hot," the three superstates can each keep their populations too busy with the war effort to be capable of thinking of ways of changing the system, even if they had the language available to them to conceive of social or political change. The three states prop each other up, even though they are periodically either mortal enemies, whipping up bitterly fanatical hatred in their populations against the foreigners, or else uneasy allies. War provides a psychologically acceptable means of destroying the surpluses, the margin which makes for comfortable living in society.

Members of the Party are expected simultaneously to be industrious, intelligent (within certain narrow limits), and efficient. At the same time, they are to be ignorant fanatics whose prevailing moods are "fear, hatred, adulation [of Big Brother] and orgiastic triumph." The fact that the Party members can simultaneously maintain this dual, contradictory state of being is due to the practice of Doublethink, a process in which a person may control his mind so that he will not even allow himself to think thoughts which are not approved by the Party. Thus the members of the Party delude themselves, as a sacred duty, into believing that Oceania is fighting a war which will certainly end victoriously and in which Oceania, by triumphing, will rule the world. To think anything else on this matter is Thoughtcrime.

When we meet Winston Smith, he is at the dangerous point where the conditioning, the Doublethink, the sense of commitment to the Party and its objectives, are breaking down. He knows it, and he knows that the thoughts he is thinking will lead him straight to his grave, or worse, at the hands of the Thought Police, but he cannot help himself. Writing in his diary, he writes, not once but over and over again, hysterically -

Down With Big Brother Down With Big Brother Down With Big Brother Down With Big Brother Down With Big Brother

From the moment when he thinks this forbidden thought, his fate is sealed. His downfall will take some time. At his place of work in the Ministry of Truth, he has the job, along with many others, of altering (really forging, though he will not admit to himself that this is what he is doing) the back issues of the London Times to bring past history into conformity with Party doctrine in the present. Thus even the past is being continuously altered by those who control it - the Party.

Winston becomes acquainted with two persons at work who are going to have a great influence on his life: Julia a twenty-six-year-old girl who is to become Winston's mistress, in part as an act of defiance of the Party, and O'Brien, a forceful member of the Inner Party, who will lead both Julia and Winston down a road of self-incrimination in search of the shadowy Brotherhood which is said to seek the overthrow of Big Brother. O'Brien will eventually betray, as he was planning to do from the beginning, both Winston and Julia.

Winston and Julia are expected to be orthodox in their thought and behavior, as both are members of the Outer Party employed in the Ministry of Truth. The Party must approve all marriages, and is suspicious of the sexual instinct and indeed of any romantic love, especially between husband and wife. This suspicion stems from the Party's perception that any attachment of one human being for another will weaken the attachment to or affection for Big Brother of the people concerned - and a good Party man or woman is expected to love Big Brother, whose picture is everywhere in the society of *1984,* though apparently nobody has seen him in person. The only sexuality grudgingly tolerated by the Party is what is called in Newspeak, "Goodsex." Goodsex is normal sexual intercourse between husband and wife only for the purpose of the procreation of children. Winston Smith had been married previously, to a fanatically loyal Party member named Katherine. They had separated, with cordial dislike for each other, after they found themselves unable to fulfill their "duty to the Party" by having children. But they have not been divorced, because the Party does not allow divorce, except in a few cases, between Party members. The Proles, who hardly count at all though they constitute the masses-nearly 85 per cent of the population of Oceania-on the other hand are not restricted at all in respect to their marital or sexual lives. "Proles and animals are free" says the contemptuous Party slogan; the Proles exist only to provide workers and soldiers for the State and to breed more soldiers and workers. But they are kept in ignorance and are not allowed to rise higher; if a Prole looks as if he might cause trouble; the Thought Police find out about him and liquidate him.

Julia works in Pornosec, a division of the Ministry of Truth which provides "literature" of a sort for the Proles to keep them out of trouble: the novels which she helps compose are written by machine, and have only six possible plots which are shuffled around to make an infinite number of combinations. This is pornographic literature which is made available to the Proles so that they will be further corrupted, as it is State policy to distract the Proles with cheap gin and limitless filthy literature. Party members who are found guilty of the vices of the flesh are severely punished.

Julia seduces Winston, not that he needs much urging once he learns that she can be trusted, that she is not a spy or an agent of the Thought Police. By entering into this clandestine relationship - they can never marry, because the Party would not allow it, especially as Winston's wife is still living - they set themselves against the Party, even though both know that such defiance, no matter how carefully they hide it, will be found out. "Thoughtcrime does not entail death: thoughtcrime is death." Winston, writing this Party slogan in his diary, perceives that he is already among the dead, for his thoughts, from the point of view of the Party, make him guilty of disloyalty. And the point of view of the Party is all important; no other way of looking at reality can be acceptable in *1984*. The initial consummation of the relationship between Winston and Julia is as much a political act of defiance against the Party as it is an act of love. But even as they rebel, Big Brother is watching them.

Big Brother is watching in the form of O'Brien, an urbane, intelligent executive in the Ministry of Truth who is a member of the Inner Party and thus several levels above Winston and Julia. He strikes up a casual social acquaintance with Winston, and in due course Winston and Julia visit him at his living quarters where, as a member of the Inner Party, he has the privilege of turning off the two-way telescreen which constantly spies on all members of the *1984* society. They denounce themselves to him as adulterers and Thoughtcriminals. Winston says that he has heard of a secret Brotherhood, whose leader is Emmanuel Goldstein, the Enemy of the People, who directs the Brotherhood in its efforts to overthrow Big Brother. But just as is the case with Big Brother, nobody has seen Goldstein in person, and it is quite probable that both Big Brother and Goldstein are creations of the Party.

Winston and Julia volunteer their services to the Brotherhood through its supposed representative, O'Brien, and they are accepted. Neither has any illusions about saving the world of the present; at most, their hope is to influence the future through present action. They will commit acts of terrorism, even murder, if necessary in support of the Brotherhood. O'Brien promises Winston that he will deliver to him a copy of Goldstein's notorious book, *The Theory and Practice of Oligarchical Collectivism*, which will explain the historical development of society down to 1984. At this, they part. "We will meet again," says O'Brien, "in the place where there is no darkness." Winston knows something of O'Brien's meaning, for he, Winston, has had a dream in which O'Brien was one of the main figures and in which this phrase was used.

The place where there is no darkness will turn out to be the brightly lit underground rooms of the Ministry of Love, where criminals are interrogated and tortured by agents of the Thought Police. For O'Brien is leading Winston on, encouraging him in his activities against the Party; it is like an elaborate game played by the members of the Inner Party, for reasons which we shall presently see. Winston and Julia have found a place free of telescreens; a cheap furnished room above an antique shop run by an old gentleman, a Mr. Charrington, in a broken-down corner of London. There, one day, as they are in bed, the Thought Police come for them. Even Mr. Charrington is revealed to be a disguised agent of the Thought Police. And in the place where there is no darkness, where Winston separated from Julia, is taken, he meets O'Brien once again.

"I will save you, Winston, I will make you perfect," O'Brien tells him. For several years Winston has been under suspicion. His smallest actions have been watched; his picture has been taken innumerable times and his voice recorded. Now he is to be "cured." The Party does not merely kill its enemies; that would be too simple. It must change their way of thinking; it must break them until they are perfect instruments of Big Brother. They may be killed after they are "perfect," according to the Party's notions of perfection. This is relatively unimportant, for it is not physical destruction of its enemies which is the Party's primary objective-it is mental and spiritual destruction.

Most of the rest of *1984* concerns Winston Smith's interrogation, torture, renunciation of his "errors," backsliding, ultimate torture, betrayal of Julia, who is the human being closest to him in the whole world, and final spiritual destruction, so complete that by the end of the book he loves Big Brother. The Party has utterly broken him. A crucial point in the understanding of what the Party wants from him is explained by O'Brien in one of the many torture sessions to which he subjects Winston. Winston provides just another excuse for the exercise of Power by the Party. Naked Power is its god, and there must be limitless opportunities to exercise that power or it will cease to exist. Winston is such an opportunity. The Party had actually made it easy for him to trap himself, foreseeing everything, because in its collective intelligence it is so much more clever than Winston. The end of Power is Power; the objective of the Inner Party is to maintain itself in power by any means which are necessary. Torture is necessary. Approximately the last third of *1984* is devoted to a sort of Socratic dialogue between O'Brien and Winston on the nature of power and on the objectives of the society. But unlike a Socratic dialogue, in which there is free exchange of views between Socrates and his students and disciples, using the process of the dialectic to arrive at truth no matter where it may lie, the dialogue between O'Brien and Winston is really a monologue in which O'Brien leads Winston on to a predetermined thought position. If the Party orders it, Winston must be prepared to believe that black is white, and that two plus two equals five.

The last part of the book, then, chronicles Winston's awful punishment at the hands of his "teacher," O'Brien, and his complete submission to the Party whose passive instrument he has become. The Party has won. He may be shot, or he may even lead a life comparatively free of supervision - but in any case, he thinks no thoughts which are not approved by the Party. He is a textbook case of a man who has been reformed by the Party. Just as the Ministry of Peace is concerned with War (War is really the Peace of the society of *1984*), so, in the Ministry of Love, where the most abominable tortures are daily inflicted on defenseless victims, the love of Big Brother for his people is made manifest. He will heal all those who have departed from the truth which the Party teaches, even if they are slowly killed in the process.

The development of the plot structure, then, of *1984* proceeds in terms of Winston Smith's decline, fall, and ultimate rescue from his thoughts of rebellion against the Party. Winston is truly dead by the end of the book, even though physically he is still alive. But when the spirit has been so thoroughly eroded and crushed, using all the techniques of a perverted science uninhibited by any laws, or safeguards of the rights of the individual, it matters little, from the point of view of the Party, whether physically he is alive or dead. He is so broken at the end that he may well kept alive, as one more self-congratulatory reminder to the Party of its triumph.

How Winston falls from grace in the Party, is broken, and is redeemed - and the political theory behind his treatment and behind the structure of society in general as well as in the particularized form represented by Winston-will be examined in detail in the succeeding sections of commentary and analysis. It should be kept in mind that the unrelieved gloom of the ending of *1984*, and the completeness of the shattering of Winston's integrity, were the work of Orwell when he was a dying man, as was pointed out in the consideration of his biography. The book is a warning, not a prediction.

JAMES BURNHAM'S THE MANAGERIAL REVOLUTION AND ITS RELATION TO ORWELL'S WORK

A rather famous book which was first published after the outbreak of World War II, was James Burnham's *The Managerial Revolution*. Burnham, a political theorist who was attempting to explain the popularity of totalitarian forms of government in the 1930s as well as the events leading up to World War II, attracted the attention of Orwell, who in 1946 published a pamphlet called *Second Thoughts on James Burnham*. The date of publication proves that Burnham's theories were much on Orwell's mind as he was preparing to write *1984*.

Orwell himself, in *Second Thoughts on James Burnham*, summarized the thesis of *The Managerial Revolutio*n as follows: "Capitalism is disappearing but Socialism is not replacing it. What is now arising in a new kind of planned, centralised society which will be neither capitalist nor, in any accepted sense of the word, democratic. The rulers of this new society will be the people who effectively control the means of production, that is, business executives, technicians, bureaucrats, and soldiers, lumped together by Burnham under the name of 'Managers.'

These people will eliminate the old capitalist class, crush the working class, and so organise society that all power and economic privilege remain in their own hands."

"The new 'managerial' societies will not consist of a patchwork of small, independent states but of great super-states grouped around the main industrial centers in Europe, Asia, and America. These super-states will fight among themselves for possession of the remaining uncaptured portions of the earth, but will probably be unable to conquer one another completely. Internally, each society will be hierarchical, with an aristocracy of talent at the top and a mass of semi-slaves at the bottom."

This, it should be remembered, is a summary of Burnham's book in Orwell's own words. The description of the future which Burnham gave, based on his explanation for the success of Hitler and Stalin, was profoundly repugnant to Orwell, who undertook to discuss and refute Burnham's book as an accurate description of the future. For Orwell, Burnham was too much in the tradition of Machiavelli and of what the Germans cynically called Realpolitik (the notion that political power in the last analysis rests only on sheer physical force, that political objectives simply cannot be attained without force). Orwell said in 1946 that Burnham's theory was "extraordinarily plausible" as an interpretation of what was actually happening at the time. But he said that it was by no means certain that the world would go in the direction which Burnham had predicted, especially if men were aware made of the awful possibilities enthusiastically outlined by such writers as Burnham. Part of Burnham's fault, in Orwell's view, is that his worship of sheer power blurred his political judgment. Further, Burnham lacked a sense of simple decency in his perception of the possibility of enslavement of the many by the few managers at the top of a society which many be described as "oligarchical collectivism."

Nevertheless, Burnham's description of man's probable future loomed large in Orwell's thinking as he wrote *1984*. Goldstein's secret Book is at once a **satire** on Burnham and an embodiment of certain ideas expressed in *The Managerial Revolution*. Therefore Burnham's writings, both the latter book and a book of essays which Burnham published in 1943 under the title, *The New Machiavellians: Defenders of Freedom*, should be considered in any serious attempt to interpret what Orwell was saying in *1984*. Basically, Orwell refuted Burnham, even while describing a society in *1984* which was akin to the society which Burnham had predicted. But Orwell was warning men, not predicting their new society.

LAW AND TOTALITARIANISM: THE LAW IN 1984

One of the most important points which Orwell made in *1984* by way of his **satire** of totalitarianism involved the changed conception of law and justice in the country of Oceania. Indeed, Orwell makes a special point of the nature of Thoughtcrime and its "antidote," Crimestop, which is the mental gymnastic by means of which a Party member may avoid the unpardonable offense of Thoughtcrime.

Western jurisprudence, whether in the common-law jurisdictions (England and the British countries generally, and the United States, whose legal institutions by and large were derived from English theory and practice) or in the civil-law jurisdictions (in countries such as Italy and France, whose legal codes are generally traceable back to Roman law), is the product of a slow evolution over the period of at least twenty-five hundred years. It takes its origin in the legal codes of the ancient Hebrews, as expressed in the Old Testament, and in the legal theory and practice of the Greeks and Romans. All of these peoples may be said to have believed in the idea that men-first some men but ultimately, under Christianity, all men, whatever their rank or wealth or station in life-had what the American Declaration of Independence calls "certain inalienable rights." Inalienable unable to be given or bargained away, that which cannot be alienated. These rights can have no validity in society unless they are actually guaranteed and if necessary enforced by law. Merely to write guarantees of human rights into a law or code is not enough, either, because unless they are enforced the rights have little meaning. But what are these "inalienable rights?"

Oversimplifying this discussion, as is necessary in order to be brief, one may say that a basic right is to be governed by a code of law which does not permit a person to be accused or convicted of a crime unless he knows at least that the act or omission (failure to act where a legal duty to act is imposed) is in fact a crime. The legal maxim is nulla poena sine lege, which is translated as: "No punishment without a law." That is, no man may be punished for breaking the law unless there is in fact a written law to be broken. The man must not be required to read all laws, but he is presumed to know the law: ignorantia legis neminem excusat, another legal maxim which means that "Ignorance of the law excuses no man."

In *1984* there is no written law, and everything is, or can be, considered a crime, at the pleasure of the State and the Party. All crimes are comprehended in one crime: Thoughtcrime. And this ultimately involves, not forbidden acts, but forbidden thoughts. Everyone knows this, though the matter is referred to infrequently. English and American law takes no account of thoughts, but only of acts or omissions. How can a man be held legally responsible for thinking prohibited thoughts? Yet this is exactly the objective of the Party, which leads to a complete and ironbound tyranny.

Certain rights which Western man has come to regard as elementary have been abolished from the society of *1984*. American law at least, following the English precedent, recognizes the rights of habeas corpus, that is, put simply, the right of a man who has been arrested or detained by the police to be brought before a magistrate or judge soon after his arrest, to be charged with a crime and held for further action or, if the police do not have enough evidence to charge him with crime, to be released immediately. In *1984*, people can be held without trial for months or years, without even being informed of the charges against them.

In *1984*, people simply "disappear," as did Winston Smith's father and mother, as did Syme, Jones, Aaronson, and Rutherford. No safeguards are imposed in the society against the most arbitrary and brutal treatment of the individual. Another fundamental right is to have personal integrity respected. But the Party not only does not respect the integrity of one's person, but violates it by design, in order to degrade men to the point where they are no longer human, but only soulless robots. This is what the Party does to Winston and Julia.

There is, of course, an ordinary criminal law in *1984*. Certain nonpolitical offenses are still defined as crimes. But they are not regarded as seriously as political offenses: murder, theft, and such crimes of violence and moral corruption as these are repressed by the Party, but not with as heavy a hand as are political offenses, all comprehended in Thoughtcrime. And ordinary criminals are treated with some favoritism by the police and the jailers of *1984*.

In short, the absence of a clearly defined written criminal law leaves punishment and imprisonment up to the whim of individuals. In the totalitarian states of the 1930s and 1940s,

Orwell saw that such procedures as imprisonment without trial, secret execution, and political assassination were used as normal instruments of state. Projecting these tendencies into the future, he believed that he could see the possibility, unless men were vigilant in the defense of their rights and liberties under written law, of a time when men would have no rights other than those granted them by a supreme Party of Government-a condition so extreme as to make human life hardly worth living.

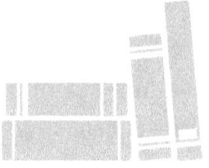

1984

TEXTUAL ANALYSIS

PART ONE, SECTIONS 1 - 3

1984 falls naturally into three Parts, with an Appendix on "The Principles of Newspeak" which is extremely important, and which will be analyzed separately in the present study. It will be compared and contrasted with Orwell's key essay, written in 1946, entitled "Politics and the English Language," an essay which contains not only the idea of Newspeak but also many of the concepts embodied more imaginatively in *1984*.

As the scenes succeed each other the novel is divided further, within each Part, into sections, for Orwell, by a technique of presenting representative scenes from the daily life of Winston Smith in *1984*, wishes to paint a picture of the effect of a totalitarian society on the individual. The technique may be called "leaping and lingering," and chronologically the action takes place over a number of months, as Winston becomes aware of the horror of his environment, seeks first to know more about it and then to change it, if necessary by violence, and finally is caught by the Thought Police and utterly destroyed as human being. Part One, containing eight sections of unequal length, deals with Winston's questioning of the system and his dawning self-awareness and introspection (which the Party discourages), as symbolized by the initial step of his keeping a private diary. Part Two, by far the longest of the three Parts, begins with Winston's serious acquaintance with Julia and then his mistaken confidence in O'Brien and his and Julia's commitment, through O'Brien, to the objectives of the secret Brotherhood in its quest for the overthrow of Big Bother. Part Two ends with the capture of the two thoughtcriminals, Winston and Julia, and their imprisonment in the cellars of the Ministry of Love where they are to be tortured. Part Two contains ten sections. Part Three, the shortest and grimmest Part, contains six sections, and deals entirely with the process of torture and brainwashing which Winston undergoes at the hands of O'Brien; it is the climatic portion of the novel. For convenience in the analysis and summary of the work, each of the three Parts will be treated separately, and further dealt with using the division into sections mentioned above.

PART ONE: SECTION ONE

Because this first section of the novel provides, through the use of **exposition**, an introduction to the major characters of *1984* as well as to some of the most important structures, ideas, and concepts of the totalitarian society which is the subject of Orwell's **satire**, it is necessary to analyze it closely.

In the opening scene of Part One, we meet Winston Smith, representative man of the society of 1984, walking into his apartment in Victory Mansions, a pretentiously named but broken-down apartment house containing too many people living too close together: a place smelling of boiled cabbage and old rags. The elevators, as is usual, due to the chronic shortage of electric power, are not working, so Winston must walk up seven flights of stairs and through narrow smelly corridors to reach his apartment.

The first thing Winston encounters, in the hallway just at the entrance, is a huge colored poster with an enormous face; and rugged face of a strong and forceful man of about forty-five with a heavy black moustache. Similar posters are on each floor, and they are drawn so that the eyes of the face on the poster seem to follow the beholder. At the bottom of the poster is the slogan, in large letters: Big Brother Is Watching You. As Winston walks slowly up the seven flights to his apartment, his varicose ulcer above his right ankle troubles him. Though he is relatively young, he is frail and not in good health, so the climb taxes his strength.

Winston is dressed in a uniform consisting of blue overalls - the uniform of a member of the Outer Party. This is to symbolize the origins of the party, which claims to be descended from the party of workers, that is, manual and factory workers, and whose philosophy, as another poster outside in the street near Victory Mansions proclaims, is called INGSOC [English Socialism]. As we shall see, the Party of which Winston Smith is a marginal member despises the manual workers, the Proles, though it adopts their dress, and its philosophy has little or nothing to do with English socialism or with any brand of socialism, no matter how loosely that elastic political term is defined.

In Winston's apartment, as he enters, there is a voice coming from a telescreen-a sort of built-in metal television screen which is a device found almost everywhere in Oceania. The voice is droning out an interminable rapid monologue about the overfulfillment of the Ninth Three-Year Plan and about pig iron.

But Winston, though he can turn it down to a whisper, cannot turn the machine off. Even turning it down might be dangerous, because it is also a transmitter, sending to some central police observation station the picture of everything and everybody in the apartment. Big Brother is indeed watching, though the individual has no knowledge about when he is being watched, but must proceed on the assumption that his every word and expression is under scrutiny by the Party.

Looking out the window, Winston can see the tumble-down houses of London, many built in the nineteenth century, interspersed with bomb craters and rows of shacks build in spaces cleared by bombs. Even the appearance of the city has been declining though Winston does not have a real standard of comparison. The only modernistic building on Winston's immediate horizon is an enormous pyramidal white concrete structure, taller than New York's Empire State Building. This is the Ministry of Truth, the propaganda ministry where Winston works and from which he has just come. This building has in huge letter on its face the three slogans of the Party: War Is Peace, Freedom Is Slavery, Ignorance Is Strength. Much of Winston's activity in this work chronicling his decline and fall will involve his learning more about the various meanings of these three slogans.

The city of London is the chief city of Airstrip One. Orwell calls England by this name for a good reason in terms of his purpose of political **satire**: he projected England's place among nations as declining after the end of World War II to the point where she is little more than an airstrip, a military and naval base, for even more powerful countries. Thus England is "the third most populous of the provinces of Oceania." Orwell does not go into more detail about the various countries which make up the superstate of Oceania which is ruled by Big Brother; for maximum specificity he limits his narrative entirely to what takes place during a few months in the lives of several individuals in the capital city of this one province, but the reader is quite able to generalize and to guess for himself what the entire country and society of Oceania is like.

Winston, on this crucial date in his life, April 4, 1984, is about to open a diary. As we have seen, it is not illegal for a citizen to keep a diary in *1984* - nothing is illegal, in terms of the violations of written law, but the all-encompassing offense of Thoughtcrime is not denounced by a written set of laws. Everyone "understands" and therefore should not expect to be told in writing what the law is. (See the discussion of "The Law in 1984" below.) But Winston's hand trembles as he begins to write in his diary. He knows that what he vaguely wants to do- to communicate with the future-is impossible. Why should the future listen to him? And what assurance does he have that the future will be any better than the present? Still, he must write. In a small, childish handwriting (Orwell adds this detail to show that most citizens in 1984 are not even used to writing, as there are other, more approved means of communications such as the Speakwrite machine), Winston begins to write in a state of fear and panic. His inner thoughts and feelings, long repressed, pour out of him. He is, one might say, in a trancelike or hysterical state, and it is his unconscious, sickened by the steady diet of violence and deceptive news fed him, which is rebelling and expressing itself. He writes of a movie (a "flick") which he had seen the previous night, in which the featured scene was a ship full of refugees being bombed in the Mediterranean, with the camera showing very graphically how people in lifeboats were then machine-gunned and blown up; "there was a wonderful shot of a child's arm going up up up right up into the air a helicopter with a camera in its nose must have followed it up and there was a lot of applause...."

As Winston writes of this brutal scene, his mind is on something quite different, though in a hidden way related at least to the brutality: an experience which he had had that very morning at his place of work in the Ministry of Truth. It was in the Records Department, and at 11:00 A.M. the people who worked in that Department were assembling for a daily ritual, the Two Minutes Hate. He had noticed a girl, about twenty-six or twenty-seven, of attractive appearance and with the sash of the Junior Anti-Sex League would around the waist of her overalls. And at this meeting for the Two Minutes Hate (a ritual which really whipped the people into a hysterical frenzy), the girl gave the impression that she was looking at Winston, sizing him up. He was afraid; she might be an agent of the Thought Police or some other kind of spy.

The girl is not the only one who will obtrude on his consciousness this day. There is an urbane, athletic-looking man whom Winston had seen perhaps a dozen times in as many years in which he had worked in the Ministry of Truth, and whom he knows only as O'Brien. He is a member of the Inner Party, wearing the uniform of black overalls which marks out this most important segment of the society of *1984*, and he is so important that nobody really knows just what his job is. Winston feels drawn to O'Brien, because his intuition tells him that O'Brien's political orthodoxy is not perfect.

O'Brien sits near Winston as the Two Minutes Hate begins on the telescreen. The Hate begins and soon the audience is, in spite of themselves, screaming at the images which appear in the telescreen with fear, rage, and hatred. Emmanuel Goldstein, the Enemy of the People, is presented denouncing the Party and Big Brother, and this is succeeded by the calming figure of Big Brother who will set all things right. The people chant rhythmically, like savages: "B-B! . . . B-B! . . B-B!" over and over again. But even as the Hate rises to a **climax**, Winston catches O'Brien's eyes, and perceives therein a flash of recognition. I am on your side, O'Brien's expression seems to say to Winston; I, too, hate them!

Back in his apartment, as he thinks of the scene that morning, Winston Smith writes uncontrollably: Down With Big Brother. He repeats it again, many times in fact. While doing this he knows that he has crossed the point of no return. They (the Thought Police, the authorities) will get him now; it is inevitable. But meanwhile he allows himself to think his own thoughts. He knows that he will be vaporized, which is the usual Party word for what happens to those who are found to be unorthodox politically. They "disappear," often with no advance warning, and often even their closest relatives do not know what happened to them nor do they dare to ask. "I don't care . . . they can shoot me. . ." Winston tells him if, inwardly, while afflicted with an awful fear as, with a knock on the door of his apartment which recalls him to "reality," the scene ends.

Comment

This initial section of Part One is a brilliant **exposition** of the world of *1984*. Its technique is that of drama, in which things are not stated to the audience or reader, but are shown through action. Part of the life which Orwell is able to impart to his characters who, after all, are political abstractions in the grip of an iron political system-especially the believability of Winston Smith-stems from Orwell's skillful and economical dramatic handling of his material. We are not told all about Winston Smith, but we seem to know him through this dramatic presentation of his character.

Since the first section of Part One raises so many issues, it may be in order here simply to analyze and comment on the more important of these:

1. Introduction of the central characters: Section One of Part One serves to introduce and partly to characterize all three of the principals of the story, Winston Smith, O'Brien, and the girl, not yet identified by name, who works in the Ministry of Truth with Winston. Though we cannot guess the connections, we know that somehow the lives of these three are to be closely related throughout the action of *1984*; Winston himself senses this, subconsciously, during the Two Minutes Hate.

2. Use of psychology; mass conditioning: We can see early that Orwell is presenting a study of Winston Smith's psychology, and through this a picture of how totalitarianism acts on a representative "average man." There is no doubt that the society which is outlined in *1984*, even in the first section of Part One, is totalitarian, though the paradoxical three slogans of the Party which tend to support this impression of the society are not yet explained. But the presentation of Winston's unconscious and semiconscious activities, his hysterical writing in his secret diary, and the state of fear in which he lives, give us an inkling that part of Orwell's interest is in the psychology of such a man as Winston. The Two Minutes Hate, with the shifting scenes of violence; the alternation of a hated object (Goldstein and the Eurasian soldiers) followed by the loved object (Big Brother), with this constantly repeated, apparently every day, shows the possibility of psychological conditioning of the people. All must love Big Brother as the embodiment of the rightness of the Party's decisions; the Two Minutes Hate, though

it seems absurd, is no more absurd than some of the torchlight processions and the inflammatory speeches, filled with hatred, which Orwell described as occurring in the totalitarian nations of the 1930s and 40s.

3. The corruption of things into empty forms: This point involves the brilliant **satire** in which Orwell shows how in all human society, but especially in totalitarian society, mere forms are retained and myths are perpetuated after the life has gone from them. Thus, the Outer Party wears the uniform of blue overalls and the Inner Party black overalls to symbolize the working-class origin of the Party, the successor to the Socialist parties of the nineteenth and early twentieth centuries. But the overalls are an empty symbol. The Party claims to have "rescued the worker" from the evils of capitalism, yet the shortage of the basic necessities of life among all subordinate classes, other than the elite of the Inner Party, has never been more acute. And it never seems to get any better. Along with the now dead symbol of the overalls goes the philosophy known in *1984* as Ingsoc-English Socialism. Whatever it is called, the actual philosophy of government of *1984* is not socialism; it is better described as Oligarchical Collectivism, as it is in fact called in the book which is purportedly written by Goldstein to explain the aims of the society of Oceania and which Winston reads before his arrest as a Thoughtcriminal.

4. The pervasive fear and hysteria in the society of *1984*: This is dramatically evidenced by the omnipresence of the telescreens, the Two Minutes Hate with its hypnotic associations, its building up of hatred of Big Brother's enemies, and its antirationalism, as well as by the furtive

nature of Winston Smith's behavior when he simply begins to write a diary, surely by normal standards not a criminal offense. But it places him in deadly peril, for it may indicate to the Thought Police who watch everybody that he has thoughts which he is hiding.

5. The conspiracy against Big Brother: The name of Emmanuel Goldstein, Thoughtcrime, and the book are first revealed here. In terms of the historical political allegory of *1984*, Goldstein represents the Russian revolutionary leader Lev Davidovich Bronstein, better known to the world by the name of Leon Trotsky, who was one of the leaders of the Russian Revolution, and was branded by his archrival Stalin as an Enemy of the People and ultimately assassinated while in exile in Mexico. Big Brother has some of the characteristics and the appearance of Josef Stalin himself. But these two figures embodying the Party and its history in *1984* are only suggestive of those they are modeled upon; Orwell, in his effort to universalize his **theme**, wanted them to stand for more than Stalin and Trotsky. He is writing about totalitarianism, and as Orwell uses them these historic actors in the development and change of a totalitarian regime may stand for other such figures.

6. The brutalization of society: Orwell presents so-called civilized society as having regressed by 1984. The machine-gunning of defenseless women and children, the showing of such scenes of brutality in the films, and the callousness of the audience watching these films are intended to show that society has gone backwards. It is less sensitive to human suffering and, as Orwell will show subsequently, the Party wants things to be this way.

7. The chronic shortage of material comforts: Just as public taste has regressed by 1984, so has the standard of living. While Ingsoc purports to have improved the lot of the ordinary man, there are not enough of the simple necessities of life to go around: food, electric power, even razor blades for a good shave. Housing is poor, old, dark, smelly, and overcrowded, Orwell, as can be inferred from his biography, was acutely conscious of the physical side of life in its less attractive aspects, and he shows Winston Smith, in the midst of such unappetizing surroundings, as a figure worn down by fear as well as by simple material deprivation.

8. The lack of clearly defined positive law in *1984:* This final point is important in terms of Orwell's critique of the nature of totalitarian government. Constitutional government, a government of laws and not of men, has clearly defined limits to its power. But in the totalitarian government of *1984* there are no limits, and the individual has no rights guaranteed to him by any constitution or code of law. Indeed, the most serious crime does not necessarily involve an overt action; Thoughtcrime, though a capital offense, may be just a thought. All of these points are further developed by Orwell, but it is necessary to be alert to their presence in the first expository section of Part One of *1984,* for they are all important to the meaning of the book.

PART ONE: SECTION TWO

This action of the second section of Part One is designed to point up the dirtiness, the squalor, and the furtiveness of daily life in the society of which Winston Smith is a part. Winston answers the knock on his door to find, not an agent of the Thought Police (actually, such an agent wouldn't have knocked but would have broken down the door), but the wife of a neighbor, Mrs. Parsons. She asks if Winston could help her out in repairing the drain of her kitchen sink, which has become blocked. (If one were to call a repairman, it might take days or he might not come at all.) Winston agrees to help and as he cleans out the filthy drain he is harassed by the two Parsons children, a boy of nine and a girl of six or seven, who are playing with toy weapons. They are already in uniform. "I'll vaporize you, I'll send you to the salt mines," the boy says to Winston Smith. They are clamoring to be taken to see the public hanging of some Eurasian war prisoners; this again shows the brutalization of society by such spectacles as mass hangings and torture of prisoners. "Nearly all children nowadays were horrible," Winston thinks to himself. For children are trained to spy, especially on their parents, and to report any indications of unorthodoxy to the authorities. Most people are now frightened of their own children, and with good reason!

There is a dream on Winston's mind as he completes the repair of the drain. Seven years previously he had dreamed that he was in a dark room, and that someone had said to him: "We shall meet in the place where there is no darkness," Gradually, it had come upon Winston that the man who had said this to him was O'Brien, but he simply does not know why O'Brien should even be on his mind; he had never spoken to him and had only seen him casually. What is "the place where there is no darkness?" Winston does not know, but he is sure the dream will come true, although he does not know how or when. He will meet O'Brien. Nothing is one's own property any more except one's private thoughts. And, as we shall see, the Party is continually working on ways to find out what a person is thinking. It may be that Winston is already the subject of an experiment along this line, although he has no knowledge of this.

As Winston returns to his apartment for a few minutes before going back to work, he thinks that he has passed his point of no return. He is already dead, for "Thoughtcrime does not entail death: thoughtcrime is death." And he has committed Thoughtcrime.

Comment

In this section, Orwell alternates further specific, and sordid, details with further abstract reflections on the part of Winston. This is still part of Orwell's dramatic **exposition**, for he is better able to show the conditions of Winston Smith's life than simply to tell about them. The blocked-up drain, the horrible children dressed in uniforms that are no doubt meant to remind one of the Hitler Youth (an organization similar to that of the Spies to which the two Parsons children belong), and the general rundown nature of the housing all suggest the decay of society.

Winston's dream involving O'Brien will not be made entirely clear until the third Part of *1984.* Briefly, however, what Orwell means to suggest-at least this seems by far the most logical interpretation-is that the Party, of which O'Brien, of course, is a major functionary, has had its eye on Winston Smith for years, even examining his facial expression to see if there is a possible lapse from orthodoxy on his part. O'Brien has been studying Winston at exhaustive length. This is proven later in the book. The dream, in other words, is not supposed to be a prophecy or to partake of the supernatural-it is simply the point at which Winston has been made subconsciously aware, perhaps by Party psychological techniques, that he is being watched. Perhaps the Party wanted him to know this. But at this time Winston does not fathom the connection between himself and O'Brien. As to the girl at the office, he is suspicious and thinks that she may be spying on him.

Winston has, in this section, begun to formulate the objectives of his revolt. He wonders how he can appeal to the future when his own work in the Records Section of the Ministry of Truth demonstrates to him that unorthodoxy in political outlook simply is vaporized; that records, even newspapers and magazines, are systematically altered by the policy of the Party, so that there will be no written record of anything in the past which the Party does not wish to have on record. But he addresses himself, in defiance of all his training and conditioning, and in defiance of Big Brother and the Thought Police, to "... the future or to the past, to a time when thought is free, when men are different from one another and do not live alone-to a time when truth exists and what is done cannot be undone ... greetings!"

As he finishes writing in his dairy, Winston notices that two fingers of his right hand are stained with ink. He washes it off; using an old-fashioned pen, again, is not illegal, but the fact that he has been doing this may set people to thinking that his behavior is odd, and this might lead to a report to the authorities that his orthodoxy is suspect. He must be on his guard constantly against the one tiny slip that will betray him.

Science in *1984* is largely the search for new and more destructive weapons, or else it is psychological research of a limited kind, aimed to increase the ability of the Party to control individual behavior and, even more important, to find some way of reading a person's thoughts at any time and against his will. As yet, the Party's efforts have not been totally successful in either area, but Orwell implies that inevitably they will succeed, given the enormous resources they are pouring into these projects. As for disinterested scientific research in pursuit of objective truth, this has vanished, along with the creation of all art worthy of the name, as it is in conflict with the objectives of the Party.

PART ONE: SECTION THREE

Section three begins with a dream sequence that provides further expository material, principally about Winston, but secondarily about the corruptive effects which the society of *1984* has on both the individual's standard of values and on his normal emotions. To achieve his effects Orwell, of course, uses the Freudian techniques of free association, the reporting of dreams, and the symbolism of dreams. These are especially appropriate given his subject, for in the totally repressed society of *1984*, where it is mortally dangerous to express one's private thoughts during waking hours, these thoughts spill over into the unconscious. It is a basic part of Freudian theory (see especially *The Interpretation of Dreams*) that material which is repressed in or by the conscious mind will find expression in dreams. This, in short, is why the various dreams which Winston Smith has are of significance in our effort to understand him.

Winston's dream is of his mother. She is a hazy memory to him, because he was only ten or eleven years old at the time she "disappeared." She was probably imprisoned without trial, or simply vaporized by the Thought Police. This is a minor point in the consideration of Winston himself, but it may prove important, because the Thought Police were likely to keep a special watch on those whose relatives had been vaporized. Winston's father, also, had disappeared, probably in one of the great purges of the 1950s. But he retains only a shadowy memory of his father. The dream sequence, at any rate, concerns his mother and infant sister, and his memory of them drowning-sinking deeper and deeper into darkening water, as they sit in the salon of a sinking ocean liner. Their deaths are terribly tragic to him in the dream. Although Winston has no idea of how his mother really died, he is sure that she died for love of him, to save him, and he is equally as sure that at the time of her death he was too selfish to understand what a sacrifice she had made. In those days, death had a certain tragic dignity, which the Party has since taken away. The thought that there was only pain today, but no dignity, crosses Winston's mind and he seems to see this "in the large eyes of his mother and his sister, looking up at him through the green water, hundreds of fathoms down and still sinking."

After this dream, the scene shifts to a place to which Winston will return frequently in his dreams: what he calls the Golden Country. It is simply landscape, with deep pools, clear, slowmoving streams in which fish swim surrounded by pasture, hedge, and forest. What is remarkable about the dream is that the "girl with dark hair." the girl at the office, is approaching him - and as she comes near, with a disdainful gesture she throws off her clothes and stands before him naked.

Winston awakens with the word "Shakespeare" on his lips, only to find that he is late to participate in the daily calisthenics (performed in front of the telescreen), which are a requirement in the lives of all the residents of Oceania. They are too much for him; he coughs, but frantically keeps on with the exercises, because they can see him, and he may be suspect if he does not do the required morning exercises with sufficient enthusiasm.

As he does the exercises, Winston thinks of the state of perpetual war in which Oceania finds itself-he cannot remember when the country has not been at war with someone - and he thinks of his mother and sister again. What is the truth? Who is Oceania actually fighting? He should know the history of Oceania but he has difficulty in remembering which country she had fought in what year. Even during the physical exercises in the morning. Winston continues his dream or trancelike state. Now he remembers the time an atomic bomb fell on Colchester (a town about sixty miles from London), apparently in a war of the 1950s. He and his father and mother had hidden in a tube (subway) station because it served as an air-raid shelter. But Winston could not remember who they were fighting. And he thinks, while doing his exercises before the telescreen, that warfare had been almost continuous since the time he was a young child. At this very moment, Oceania is in alliance with Eastasia, and at war with Eurasia. But Winston knows that this alignment of the great Powers of the world is only temporary, although it is Party doctrine that the alliance is absolutely permanent and that the Eurasians are monsters for wickedness (Eurasia probably encompassing Russia and Eastern Europe), because only four years earlier, in 1980, Oceania had been at war with Eastasia and in alliance with Eurasia. But the terribly frightening thing to Winston - and it is a point which Orwell made much of both in *1984* and in many of his other books - is that the concept of objective truth, especially historical truth, had been made obsolete. In *1984* the truth is what the Party says it is at the moment. Indeed, it is part of Winston's job to alter the truth. The life of the Party and its members is thus based on a form of "reality control" - deliberate lying both to others and to oneself - called doublethink in Newspeak. "Who controls the past controls the future: who controls the present controls the past." Of all the Party slogans which serve as a substitute for original thought, this is perhaps the most important for an understanding of *1984*. Winston, before the exercises are concluded, has another daydream. This time it is about the past which according to the official Party history (or the myth which the Party has created to help keep itself in power), consisted in the 1930s and 1940s of fabulous creatures called Capitalists, who wore top hats and oppressed the people. But of course IGSOC had ended the corrupt rule of the capitalists - the Party had done everything for the people and for civilization, even claiming to have invented airplanes. And how can anyone disprove the claims of the Party, when all information is controlled by Party apparatus?

Just once, Winston thinks to himself, he had had documentary evidence of the falsification of history. But before Winston can think of this further, he is recalled to where he is by the instructress of the physical education session who shouts at him: "6079 Smith W! Yes, you! Bend lower, please! You can do better than that." Winston does not dare to show even the least resentment at this, and as the scene ends he is a pathetic but somewhat ludicrous figure doing the exercises exactly as ordered.

Comment

This section is a further presentation of Winston's place in his society interspersed with three brief but revealing dream sequences which are so important, the second one especially, that they should be given special attention. This may be called The Dream of the Golden Country. It will recur not only throughout *1984* but in at least one other work of Orwell as well: *Coming Up for Air*, in which the middle-aged hero, George Bowling, frequently thinks about a place which he had discovered in his boyhood-a place of deep, hidden pools with fine fish swimming peacefully in them, not known to many people and therefore unspoiled. What the Golden Country means to Winston Smith will become apparent as the book unfolds, but for the present it is sufficient to say that it means something so basic to Winston, and to Orwell, that it goes far towards explaining them.

Winston dreams of the girl in the office; this is less complex than the Golden Country. He desires her, but as yet has not admitted this to himself consciously, as he is afraid that she may be a spy. In his dream he meets her in the Golden Country, and he wakes up, incongruously, with the word "Shakespeare" on his lips. But perhaps this is not so incongruous after all; Shakespeare is the greatest writer in the English language, and one of the three or four supreme creators of world literature. But in the environment of *1984*, literature not only does not flourish, but it is being systematically destroyed. The Party realizes that the language used by great literature can lead to the formulation of unorthodox thoughts. Hence, literature is being abolished, and the rich language of Shakespeare and his literary successors is being converted into a kind of basic English called Newspeak, which aims to make political unorthodoxy difficult if not impossible by taking away all peripheral, suggestive, and connotative meanings from words. If the concepts for the expression of unorthodox thoughts are taken away, how then can the thoughts themselves exist? So the Party reasons. Of course, the whole idea of changing the language to make unorthodoxy impossible is an exaggeration. But Orwell takes the whole matter quite seriously, as we shall see in considering his essay "Politics and the English Language."

Winston, then, in this section of Part One, expresses in a dream his sense of guilt, especially about his mother, and his longing for the Golden Country; he also shows that he is desirous of the girl whom he has begun to notice at his place of work. He is a man without a center to his life, and a man who does not seem to have much understanding of the actual circumstances of his environment, though he is profoundly unhappy in that environment. But he has no clear standard by which he can compare his present circumstances with anything in the past, for the past has deliberately been blurred.

1984

TEXTUAL ANALYSIS

PART ONE, SECTIONS 4-8

....

In this section, we see Winston Smith at work in the Ministry of Truth. His work is divided into two related kinds of activity: (1) the systematic alteration of newspapers and magazines, under Party orders, to bring the Past into conformity with current Party doctrine in the Present, and (2) the outright fabrication or forgery of history, for political ends.

We see Winston, during this working day, engage in both kinds of activity; it might be subtitled, therefore: "One day in the life of a good Party man." Another function of this section is to develop the concept of the new and abbreviated jargon of Newspeak, used in the offices of the government of Oceania. This language helps to distort reality and render it more acceptable. Winston has to "rectify" four printed news items from the Times (no doubt the Times of London). As an example, he receives a message in his office saying; "times 3.12.83 reporting bb dayorder doubleplusungood refs unpersons rewrite fullwise upsub antefiling." The explanation of this message of course has to do with the rewriting of Big Brother's Order for the Day of December 3rd, 1983, which "makes reference to nonexistent persons" [unpersons]. An "unperson" in Newspeak is one who has somehow fallen into political disgrace and been purged. He is not only killed or imprisoned, but the essential treatment of him, as far as the Party is concerned, is that he shall be rendered nonexistent, as though he had literally never existed, by having all references to him in newspapers and other written documents deleted. This way, there can be no martyrs and no rallying points for those who might become enemies of the Party. The suspect and the disaffected simply are vaporized and become unpersons. Winston knows that this is his own probable fate. For Winston is no longer a "good Party man."

A man named Withers had been praised in Big Brother's order. Then suddenly he had fallen into disgrace and disappeared, with no reason given, as was usual in *1984*. He is most probably dead. But it is not enough to kill him, for whatever reason; even his image must be destroyed. This is Winston's job, along with that of his immediate colleagues.

Instead of rewriting Big Brother's speech so that it will denounce Withers instead of praise him, Winston decides to write a totally new speech, unconnected with Withers and his fate. Winston thus fabricates, without a shred of objective fact, the story of a Party "hero" by the name of Comrade Ogilvy. This is sheer forgery, but as it will serve the ends of the Party it would be considered right and true by the Party. Winston dictates into the Speakwrite the story of Ogilvy, who at the age of three had refused all toys except a drum, a submachine gun, and a model helicopter. At six he joined the Spies, at eleven, denounced his own uncle to the Thought Police, and at twenty-three he died gloriously by jumping into the water from his helicopter, weighting his body with his machine gun, as he was carrying important despatches and was being pursued by the Eurasian enemy.

Comrade Ogilvy, Big Brother concludes in his speech, was absolutely single minded in his devotion to the Party. He did not drink or smoke, had no recreations except physical exercise to keep his body in shape, did not marry as he thought marriage and the care of a family would detract from his 24-hour-a-day devotion to duty, and had no subjects of conversation except the principles of Ingsoc.

Winston has created this man from nothing. Even while this process of deliberate forgery is proceeding, the writer, by the process of Doublethink, is able to convince himself that the lies he is telling are actually the truth: they are the truth because they serve the aims of the Party, and therefore must be true.

Comment

Winston's dislocation and falsification of reality in furtherance of the Party's aims may seem a fantastic exaggeration, but ultimately the process is psychologically believable. Comrade Ogilvy is created because the rank and file of the Party must have such heroes, just as they must have a Leader to worship (Big Brother) and an Enemy of the People to hate (Emmanuel Goldstein). Comrade Ogilvy has never existed in the present, but through Winston's act he now exists in the past, and exists on the same evidence as Charlemagne or Julius Caesar, that is, the evidence of written history. Lest the fabrication of Comrade Ogilvy be thought of as too extreme, we might consider the following news item, which actually appeared in the New York Times, Sunday, April 7, 1963, on page 19 of section one. It is worth some thought, because of its implications for an understanding of some of the tendencies which Orwell was exaggerating for the purposes of **satire** in *1984:*

[Sunday, April 7, 1963 p. 19]

All Red Virtues Meet In Martyr

Chinese Soldier is Survived by Best-Selling Diary

Special to the New York Times

Hong Kong, April 2, [1963]-Communist China's newspapers and magazines are busily immortalizing a young soldier who is said to have been, before his accidental death last year, a paragon of all the Communist virtues.

The young martyr, Lei Feng, meets all the specifications of the ideal Communist described in the various manifestos of Peking. He sounds somehow unreal, but has been given a flesh-blood character with the publication of his photo. Not only was Lei Feng a good Communist, a selfless worker and an efficient soldier, but also he put down his thoughts in a diary, which has become the Chinese equivalent of a best seller.

"Shining Image" Inspires

The following comment appeared in *China Youth Daily*, a Peking publication:

"The shining image projected by Lei Feng, a youth of New China, has produced a widespread and profound impact upon the broad masses of youth in our municipality.

"With Lei Feng held up as their example, many youths work, study, and live the way Lei Feng did. Hence the emergence of a number of new men and new deeds.

Hsinhua, Chinese press agency, reported that Lei Feng was born to a poor peasant family in 1940. His father was killed by the Japanese. His mother hanged herself after she was raped by a landlord.

The boy was rescued from the brink of death by the arrival of the Communists in his native village in Hunan Province. He accused the landlord who had caused the death of his mother, and saw the landlord executed.

Lei Feng worked his way up through the Young Pioneers and the Young Communist League, and joined the army in 1959.

In his diary he wrote: "I, a homeless orphan looking after pigs, have at last become a soldier of the national defense army! I really do not know what to say. I must live up to the expectations of the party."

Through Fire For Party

When he joined the Communist party he wrote: "I am a Communist party member and a servant of the people. For the sake of the party's and people's undertakings, I am even willing to plunge into a sea of fire and climb up a mountain full of knives."

As a squad leader Lei Feng learned the trade of a barber in his spare time, so that he could cut the hair of his men. He mended the clothes of the other soldiers and took only one uniform a year instead of the two he was allowed.

Hsinhua declared: "The main reason why Lei Feng was able to become a true Communist soldier was because he persisted indefatigably in studying the works of Chairman Mao, listening to Chairman Mao's words, doing things according to Chairman Mao's directives and becoming Chairman Mao's good soldier."

Lei Feng died when a comrade drove a truck into a wooden pole, which struck him on the head.

(c) 1963 by the New York Times Company. Reprinted by permission.

It should be kept in mind that Orwell was not simply satirizing what he thought of as Communist totalitarianism in *1984* and in *Animal Farm*; he was attacking all forms of totalitarianism, because he believed them to be profoundly wrong and destructive to mankind. But this particular equating of Comrade Ogilvy and Lei Feng is not farfetched. Lei Feng, on such scanty evidence as is available primarily in newspaper reports from China, seems to be something new: a manufactured culture hero and political ideal; a point of focus for the emotions of the masses.

Did Lei Feng exist? The answer to that may be that he exists to serve the aims of the Chinese Communist Party; therefore he exists, though he may never have existed in the flesh. Perhaps a writer created him just as Winston Smith created Comrade Ogilvy. The point of this comparison of Comrade Ogilvy and Lei Feng is simply that Orwell had an uncanny sense of the political tendencies of his age, especially in certain quarters of the world, and that some of the things he predicted in *1984* have already come to pass. But the major points have not yet lived up to his predictions, because by making such predictions it was really his intention to prevent such things from coming about-by warning the nations of the West and making them aware of these tendencies.

PART ONE: SECTION FIVE

Winston meets various men who in different ways represent the dehumanized society of *1984* in this section: Syme, who works in the Research Department of the Ministry of Truth and has a burning interest in Newspeak; Parsons, who is outgoing and jovial, and who is Winston's neighbor in Victory Mansions and makes a fetish of community activities and athletics on behalf of the Party. While Winston talks with Syme and Parsons (it is significant that we never learn their first names), an announcement from the Ministry of Plenty appears on the telescreen.

The announcement concerns the winning of the "battle for production" in Oceania, and the speaker tells of the overfulfilled norms of production. Statistics pour out of the telescreen, about more and better production of houses, food, ships, guns, clothes - and the reduction of disease and insanity. Yet Winston's stomach, as well as his mind, tell him that all the announcements are utter lies, that he never really has enough to eat, and that even the simplest necessities of life are in short supply. People do not even look healthy, so how can there be such abundance? Housing is dark, old, in ill repair, and crowded. And Winston, as he tells Parsons that he has no extra razor blades and that he has been using the same blade for six weeks, thinks of Mrs. Parsons and her two horrible children. In a year or two, he thinks, the children will beg denouncing their own father and mother to the Thought Police.

As they talk, Winston guards even his facial expression. He knows that to look doubtful when a new victory of the Party is announced is a punishable offense, and Winston does not want to be caught committing facecrime, as it is called in Newspeak.

Comment

In this section are developed two rather different concepts: the first has to do with orthodoxy of thought and language in a totalitarian society, while the second concerns the permanent shortage of all material comforts and goods in the society of Oceania. The theory of Newspeak is explained to Winston by Syme, who is an expert working on the Eleventh Edition of the Newspeak Dictionary. While it will be further elaborated in Orwell's Appendix to *1984* and his essay "Politics and the English Language," the essence of the theory is the abolition of all **connotations** of words, narrowing the possible range of thought so that, as Syme tells Winston enthusiastically, "In the end we shall make thought-crime literally impossible, because there will be no words in which to express it. Every concept that can ever be needed will be expressed by exactly one word, with its meaning rigidly defined and all its subsidiary meanings rubbed out and forgotten."

1984 has been compared, as an anti-Utopia and as a work of political **satire**, to Swift's *Gulliver's Travels*. There is great similarity in the philosophical analysis of language in both works; especially in Book III of *Gulliver's Travels*, Swift shows how language may be corrupted. Readers may wish to consult Orwell's essay on Swift - but the point is that both writers, who say only too clearly the possibilities of corruption inherent in man's nature, also saw that one of the ways to corrupt his language, so that disagreeable actions and topics, not to mention sheer barbarism, may be smothered in a cloud of words. Syme explains, with relish, that such a word as "freedom" can have its **connotations** abolished by action of the Party, until all that is left is the one rigid **denotation** which has little to do with the abstract concept of the rights of man or of political freedom. Thus, even a dictionary, such as the *Eleventh Newspeak Dictionary* which Syme is helping to edit, becomes a political document.

As to literature, by the year 2050 Syme predicts that the great English classics: Chaucer, Shakespeare, Milton, and the others, will have been changed into something contradictory to what they had previously been. Great literature is subversive to the Party, because it relies on the connotations of words expressive of the clearest as well as the most delicate shades of meaning-to express the exact meaning of a great mind with precision. The Party is against precision in language because this militates against the process of Doublethink. Further, great literature is expressive of a world view which will not be that of the Party, and on this ground alone could not be tolerated by the authorities.

Winston realizes with a flash of insight that while Syme is sound and orthodox in his views, he will one day be vaporized. "He is too intelligent," thinks Winston. As for Parsons, he is merely stupid and unfeeling, and therefore, thinks Winston, he will survive. In the canteen, as Winston thinks these thoughts, there is a man speaking to someone rapidly and monotonously-sounding almost as if he were a quacking duck. This illustrates duckspeak; under the principles of Doublethink, the word has two conflicting meanings-as applied to an enemy, it means abuse, for quacking like a duck is not to speak in a human voice. But applied to an orthodox Party member, it is praise, for it means that the man is speaking pure Party slogans untouched by thought; he is 100 per cent "sound" in his doctrine and therefore does not need to think.

Winston here avoids the glance of the mysterious girl from the fiction-writing department, the one whom he thinks may be a spy. At the same time he thinks dangerous thoughts: why, he asks himself, is there always a shortage of everything despite the announcements of glorious victories by the Party on the production front?

PART ONE: SECTION SIX

Winston, in this section, writes in his diary about a degrading sexual experience, and in doing so shows why the Party does everything it can to distort and dirty the sexual instinct, so that at best it is only grudgingly tolerated between husband and wife, for the purpose of breeding additional soldiers and workers for the Party. Three years previous to the time of his writing about the experience in his diary, Winston had gone with a Prole woman who was a prostitute, in a broken-down section of town, to her basement room. She used make-up and perfume, something which no woman Party member would ever do. This assignation, of course, was forbidden, but Winston felt that the worst he could get for this was five years in prison or a forced-labor camp, and besides, he suspected that the Party secretly did not mind if its members engaged in illicit sexual relations as an outlet for instincts which could not altogether be suppressed. But the cardinal condition would be that such relations further degrade the Party member and fill him with self-loathing, and this is exactly what had happened to Winston Smith. Promiscuity between Party members amounts to treason, but such a relationship as Winston had had with a despised woman of the Proles was much less serious.

Winston had been married to Katharine, also a Party member (Party members could marry only within the Party, after approval by a committee). The marriage had been barren, and they had been allowed to separate after fifteen months because there were no children, though the Party did not permit divorce. According to the chronology of *1984,* Winston and his wife had separated about 1973 or 1974. She was, in Winston's view, "the most stupid, vulgar, empty mind that he had ever encountered." While she hated the sexual aspect of marriage, she said that they must stay married as long as there was a chance of their producing a child for the Party. But as this did not happen, they separated, and Winston had lived celibate ever since, except for a few sordid **episodes** like the one with the Prole woman recorded in this section in his diary.

Comment

Orwell here and elsewhere, as in *Coming Up for Air*, equates sexuality and politics; in his view, much political fanaticism and hysterical hatred of foreigners, spies, thought-criminals, etc., was due to the repression or perversion of normal sexuality, which by and large he favored and even praised (his novel *Keep the Aspidistra Flying* revolves around the triumph of the middle-class values, of normal marriage and the raising of a family as a symbol of the affirmation of life).

But in this section of *1984* he implies that the Party has tried to pervert normal sexuality, because it perceives that through the sexual relationship people form alliances which are apart from the Party, and therefore are suspect. This leads to the succeeding scenes where Winston and Julia, both Party members (this is the unpardonable thing), are adulterers, initially as an act of political revolt against Big Brother. The Party has little reason to fear the kind of joyless, furtive experience Winston has had with the Prole prostitute; he himself is filled with self-loathing by it, which is just what the Party would like.

PART ONE: SECTION SEVEN

In Section seven, Winston continues to question the system and thereby to commit Thoughtcrime. He reviews in his own mind - this by way of further **exposition** on the part of Orwell - the history, or better, the mythology which is the foundation of Ingsoc and of the Party. "If there is hope," Winston writes in his diary, "it lies in the Proles." The Proles, however, live a life devoid of general ideas or of the realization that they are being exploited and that they could tear the Party to pieces if they chose. They are distracted by films, synthetic gin, sex (for the Party encourages them to have many children), gambling and sport - "bread and circuses." If a Prole shows any sign of becoming troublesome, he is found out and eliminated by the Thought Police. Meanwhile, there is a whole corrupt underworld of criminals in the Prole sections of London, which the Party tacitly encourages. Prostitution and drug addiction go unpunished in their cases-because to the Party, ordinary crimes are of little importance, and even benefit its ends by keeping the Proles corrupt. The serious crimes are political crimes.

Winston, in this scene, recalls an actual documentary piece of evidence proving the Party's deliberate falsification of history. This is the case of three well-known early revolutionaries: Jones, Aaronson, and Rutherford. Winston knows, from a page of the Times which had come into his possession, that they had made confessions in one of the purge trials about 1966 which were entirely lies, and Winston believes that this one fact could destroy the Party if its true significance were made known.

Comment

This section really has two functions: it develops the situation of the Proles who, as the Party slogan has it, are "free" because they are largely ignored, though they are numerically the largest component of society, and it also further elaborates on the effects of Doublethink and the forgery of history. This second function is related to the fates of Jones, Aaronson, and Rutherford, whom the Party purged as traitors, briefly rehabilitated them, and then executed them as a warning. The past changes continuously, and thus it was not what Jones, Aaronson, and Rutherford had done which was important; it was what the Party said they had done. At their trial, they had confessed that they had secretly flown to Eurasian soil to betray military secrets of Oceania to the Eurasian General Staff. But Winston has seen with his own eyes the torn page of the Times of that date on which they were supposed to have been in Eurasia, and which contained a photograph of the three men in New York. Thus, their confessions are proved photographically to be lies. In the light of what happens to Winston later in the Ministry of Love, when he himself undergoes much the same treatment as the three whose confessions he now knows to be false, it is very possible that the Party had actually "planted" the Times page so that Winston would see it. For if the Party says that two and two made five, you must to believe it, thinks Winston. But he is not prepared to believe, or to reject the evidence of his senses, in the case of Jones, Aaronson, and Rutherford or in any other cases. This is his great crime, in the eyes of the Party. He writes in his diary, as this section ends: "Freedom is the freedom to say that two plus two make four. If that is granted, all else follows." He understands How (that is, how the Party operates, and how it distorts reality for political ends). But he does not understand Why (why the Party does this). He is to learn the answer to the second part of his question in the torture rooms of the Ministry of Love. The Party loves him, and therefore will make him perfect, even if it kills him - and Winston already realizes that this will be his fate.

PART ONE: SECTION EIGHT

Winston is engaged, in this section, in trying to check up on the truth of the official Party histories of the age prior to the Ingsoc Revolution. He does his research in a low dive in a Prole section of London, buying an old man a few beers and asking him what it was really like under what the Party histories would call the iron heel of capitalist-imperialist oppression by the capitalists in their top hats, and their hangers-on such as the lawyers and men of religion. But Winston finds out nothing, certainly not whether life was better or worse in the old days than it is in 1984. He just feels that it must have been better. As this section, and Part One, ends, Winston is thinking of renting a sort of hideaway in the Prole section of town: a cheap furnished room over an old antique store which stocks some of the odd luxuries and objects of art which had existed before the Revolution, and which is owned by an old man, a Mr. Charrington, though the name on the shop window is not Charrington but Weeks. He knows that it will be dangerous to rent such a place. In the area near Mr. Charrington's shop Winston sees the girl with the black hair from the office. Now he knows that she must be a spy, for the meeting cannot be a coincidence. The thought occurs to him that he should bash in her skull and run, but instead he simply goes home, thinking what it will be like when the Thought Police come for him at night. As Part One ends, Winston is meditating on the meaning of the Three Slogans of the Party. But he still does not understand them.

Comment

This section also shows the distortion of the past and indeed of reality by the Party. By providing an oversimplified and largely false picture of the twentieth-century capitalist society prior to the Revolution, the Party aims to persuade the populace, especially the Proles, that the present is vastly superior in terms of material well-being. But the history which all good Party members are supposed to read and believe as an article of faith is indeed garbled; it mixes up various features of the past, which, if they existed at all, properly belonged to the Middle Ages rather than to the twentieth century. The capitalist, always wearing a top hat (which some wealthy men and public figures did indeed wear on important occasions in the past), blends into the remembrance of the jus primae noctis (meaning, literally, "law of the first night" - the supposed law which gave the feudal landholder the right to sleep with the daughter of a tenant, serf, or villein on the first night after she has been married to one of her own class). But it is a historical question whether this custom ever really existed at any time; the point is that the Party does not care whether it existed, but rather uses its supposed existence to prove the superiority of the "free" present to the oppressive past. Yet at the same time, by the principles of Doublethink, freedom is among the worst of evils: "Freedom is Slavery." As to Mr. Charrington's antique shop, and the dingy room above it which Winston thinks of renting, because it has no telescreen (he imagines), this symbolizes an earlier, half-forgotten London, as to the bells of the London churches which have disappeared or been converted into war museums-yet Winston hears the song of the bells in his mind. He is looking for an escape. But there is to be none for him.

PART ONE: SUMMARY

By the end of Part One, Orwell has developed and illustrated the structure of the society of Oceania. Of course, as was observed earlier, it is an exaggeration - but a serious one. The pattern of the eight sections of Part One, which contain the dramatic **exposition** of *1984*, is as follows:

Section One

The three slogans of the Party, the three classes of society, and Winston's initial act of thought-crime, and his beginning of a diary and meeting with the girl with the black hair and with O'Brien. This section is by far the most important of Part One.

Section Two

A dream sequence in which Winston's true feelings spill over from his unconscious. A picture of the rundown, sordid material environment and of the way in which the system prevents even the children.

Section Three

A further dream sequence and the initial idea of the Golden Country which Winston is seeking; an explanation of Doublethink.

Section Four

Winston's work in the Ministry of Truth; the systematic falsification of history; the creation of persons who never existed in reality as symbols for the Party's ends, and conversely the making of persons who did exist once in the flesh into "unpersons."

Section Five

Winston's meeting with two representative dehumanized members of the Outer Party, Syme and Parsons, who show what the system does to most people; an explanation of Doublethink and of Newspeak.

Section Six

The Party's systematic perversion and degradation of love between husband and wife and of the basic normal sexual instinct, which are incompatible with the aims of the Party. This is treated concretely, in terms of a harrowing and sordid experience of Winston himself. Winston's marriage and its failure.

Section Seven

Documentary proof that the Party forges history. The situation of the Proles, in which Winston finds some hope if only the Proles can become conscious, self-aware beings. The story of Jones, Aaronson, and Rutherford, and the way in which it illustrates the Party's twisting of reality to fit its needs of the moment.

Section Eight

Winston's attempt to find a hiding place within his society; his further consciousness of the girl with the black hair, to whom he knows that his fate is already linked in some mysterious way, though she is probably a spy.

    Each of these sections may be said to illustrate the projection by Orwell of what he saw as a mode, a tendency, or an attitude of the present (approximately 1950): the use of unthinking and unthoughtout political slogans; the repression of reality and its presence only in dream states; falsification and exaggeration of objective historical reality in support of a political theory; the use of the secret police, terror, violence, intimidation, and systematic moral corruption of a population to make the people easier to handle; the dehumanization of man; the perversion of normal and healthy sexuality for political ends; the fruitless attempt of the individual to find a place of rest, a hiding place, within a totally immoral and corrupt society. Orwell was warning his contemporary reading public against all of these tendencies, and was saying in effect that if people were not made aware of these things, by 1984 or at any rate sometime soon, the exact year being unimportant, the natural development of these perverted tendencies would result in a society similar to that ruled by Big Brother and the Party.

1984

TEXTUAL ANALYSIS

PART TWO

....

While Part One has described Winston Smith's increasing urge, arising partly from his subconscious, against his society which he intuitively feels (but cannot prove) is rotten to the core, Part Two deals with the progressive acting out of Winston Smith's hostility to the Party and to Big Brother. We already know that the revolt will lead nowhere but to the torture chambers of the Thought Police; everyone who revolts is caught sooner or later, and Winston has already accepted an image of himself as an "unperson" who, if he is fortunate, may at least be able to effect small changes in a future which he will never, personally, see. The form his revolt will take is partly conditioned by the opportunity which presents itself, in this section, when the girl with the black hair suddenly and unexpectedly thrusts into his hand, at work, a crumpled scrap of paper ... and when Winston looks at it, the only words written on it are: "I love you."

Comment

The difficulties of simply meeting people in *1984* are highlighted in this section. Since telescreens and hidden microphones are everywhere, people must exercise the greatest caution if they even wish to meet socially, as the presumption of the Party is that a meeting of any kind is suspect until proven innocent. The Party wants to keep people apart. A romantic attachment between Party members is especially dangerous as indicating that the people concerned are more committed to each other than to the advancing of the Party's aims.

Arranging a meeting with the girl is difficult; Winston does not know her name, or where she lives, or even in what part of the Ministry of Truth she works. He does not dare to ask directly. Sending a letter is out of the question; all letters are opened by security agencies, so that most people don't even bother to write letters any more. This section, then, is a further **exposition** of the effect which a completely totalitarian society has on the individual's everyday existence. Even the kind of revolt contemplated by Winston takes much energy and perseverance. They finally meet in the canteen in the Ministry of Truth, for about thirty seconds, and arrange a further meeting on the "outside" right near a monument dedicated to Big Brother, where there are many telescreens but where crowds of people usually congregate so that recognition by the Thought Police would be difficult. In turn, at this meeting in Victory Square, they take advantage of the 7:00 P.M. rush hour to arrange a further meeting in the country the following Sunday. In the background, on Victory Square, as they make these plans, is a procession of Eurasian war prisoners, bedraggled-looking and chained together - they are on the way either to be executed or to become inmates of forced-labor camps. Thus, Winston and the girl, whose name he still does not know, finally arrange to meet, and though no word has been spoken between them except to arrange the meeting - they do not dare speak - they both know that they have placed themselves in mortal danger.

PART TWO: SECTION TWO

On a Sunday, Winston and the girl meet; the season is May, and the train has taken them from the smoky and dusty London of the Party to at least a temporary rural freedom. Winston finally discovers the girl's name: Julia. Julia fulfills Winston's dream (see Part One, Section Three, above) doubly - the dream of the Golden Country, and the dream of her throwing off her clothes before him. For the country she has led him to is the Golden Country, and he recognizes it from his dream. The significance of this symbol will be further discussed in a brief consideration of *Coming Up for Air*; it seems to have a very private and special meaning for George Orwell, as well as for his fictional creations. Julia becomes Winston's mistress. And this is, as Orwell himself says, a political revolt as much as it is a sexual act.

Comment

The equating of sexuality and politics here may seem bizarre, but as Orwell has developed the subject in *1984,* in *Coming Up for Air, Keep the Aspidistra Flying*, and in certain of his essays, such as "Raffles and Miss Blandish" (1984), ostensibly, a remarkable criticism of detective literature, but with a purpose, as with most things written by Orwell, in part political. It is his thesis that one of the techniques by which a dictatorship attempts to control its people is by perverting normal sexuality. Orwell was actually conservative in this respect-for him, "middle-class respectability" was actually desirable if it included healthy rather than sterile and perverted and repressed sexuality. Nowhere is this more clear than in *Keep the Aspidistra Flying*. While it is true that the relationship of Julia and Winston Smith is largely on the physical level, Orwell does not think that such a relationship is necessarily immoral, given the corruption of the society surrounding the lovers. The Party knows well enough that repression of the kind inflicted on its adherents dams up the normal sexual instinct, and issues instead in fanaticism, sadism, and hatred. We learn in this section that Julia is no innocent girl by conventional standards; she has had relations with other men who were Party members. Even a member of the Inner Party, she hints, might have taken her as his mistress if he only thought he could get away with it; they were by no means as orthodox as they make out, according to Julia. But Julia is the physical woman; she is intelligent but not at all intellectual in the sense of leading the examined or self-analytic life. Ideology bores her, even as Winston is fascinated by it. However, the physical revolt of sex she does understand and appreciate. It is significant in Orwell's characterization of her that he never allows her to become other than something of a stereotype. Winston learns that her name is Julia in this section; he never learns her last name. She is not so much a unique human being here as she is a sex object.

PART TWO: SECTION THREE

During May, Winston and Julia meet a number of times in various hiding places. Julia is very experienced at concealment, and she knows that they cannot use a hideout more than twice. She tells Winston something of her past history, but it becomes clear that she is in revolt against the Party on personal and not ideological grounds. Perhaps her consciousness of sexuality has something to do with the Department of the Ministry of Truth in which she is employed; she works in Pornosec, which is concerned with writing, by machine, pornographic novels for distribution among the Proles in order to corrupt them. Winston, in turn, tells Julia of his married life, and of his repressed urge to push his wife, Katharine, over a cliff one day when they were alone. Julia seems more cheerful about life in general than Winston, but it is clear that she is no thinker and that abstract discussion bores her.

Comment

This section further develops the character of Julia, and also of Winston; the clear distinction between the minds of the two should be kept before the reader, and also the relative shallowness of Julia's revolt. Later, when they are both arrested by the Thought Police, as they know is inevitable, it will be Julia who will "confess" first, and confess abjectly and completely. Orwell implies that the reason for Julia's recantation - an almost textbook case of the success of Party brainwashing - is that her revolt is almost entirely physical. She has not thought very much about the political implications of the Party's doctrines or activities, and when Winston reads to her from Goldstein's *The Theory and Practice of Oligarchical Collectivism*, Julia goes to sleep, even though it is "the Book" which contains an explanation of the system of *1984*.

There is just a suggestion in the book that Winston and Julia are, so to speak, a modern Adam and Eve; that Orwell was using this archetypal concept to portray those who are in an environment basically hostile or foreign to them, and who rather suddenly become self-aware. But it is Julia who is, like Eve, "the weaker vessel." And there is no hint in *1984* that either Julia or Winston can ultimately be saved, in any conceivable religious sense of the term salvation. "What happens to you here [in the Ministry of Love] is forever," Winston is told by O'Brien as he undergoes scientific tortures of the most painful variety. Winston and Julia haven't a chance of escaping.

PART TWO: SECTION FOUR

Winston rents the dingy furnished room over Mr. Charrington's antique shop, and arranges to meet Julia there. He knows that it is folly for a Party member to do such a thing, and increases his chances of being found out quickly. But the temptation of having a hiding place where he can meet his mistress more frequently than had been possible is too much for Winston. The two, Winston and Julia, know that they are "intentionally stepping nearer to their graves." At this time, preparations for the Hate Week-a sort of expanded Two Minutes Hate-are going forward and their love affair is interfered with. But they do meet at the room as frequently as they are able to. And they are surrounded by symbols; symbols of an age that has been and symbols of an age that will be, Winston thinks.

Comment

Throughout this section there are a number of objects or occurrences which appear to have an import beyond the merely literal: the glass and coral paperweight, the rats, the **rhyme** "Oranges and lemons, say the bells of St. Clement's," and the song sung by the coarse Prole woman in the yard below the location of Mr. Charrington's shop. These are all to recur throughout the book, building up symbolic meanings.

The glass paperweight: "Frozen" in it permanently is a small piece of pink coral. Winston is fascinated by the paperweight and purchases it from Mr. Charrington's meager stock of antiques. It symbolizes, within the terms of the book, the times which had been and which had been liquidated by the Party. The paperweight seems to be a small, self-contained, and sealed world. It is aesthetically beautiful, not useful; therefore such an object is suspect by the Party, which pretends to value economic efficiency and usefulness only (while at the same time, by the principles of Doublethink, encouraging incredible waste). At the end of Part Two, the paperweight is wantonly smashed by a soldier in the service of the Party's secret police, symbolizing the end of Winston's attempt to enter into a private world away from Party discipline.

The rats: Julia sees a rat scurrying out of sight in the room, and casually throws a shoe at it. But when she tells Winston, he nearly faints. Everyone has an absolutely irrational fear the terror of something, as O'Brien will tell Winston later. Winston's great fear is rats; this will be used against him later by the Party in the cellars of the Ministry of Love.

The coarse Prole woman and the cheap popular song is he sings: "It was only an 'opeless fancy. . . ." She symbolizes to Winston at least an affirmation of life; her whole life has been the almost mindless breeding of children and routine housework, yet she can sing. And the song, though it is a perfectly tawdry one, composed by machine in the Music Department of the Ministry of Truth, does symbolize perhaps Winston's dreams of a better world, for it, too, will recur in the novel.

The luxuries (coffee, sugar, etc.) Julia brings to the room: These simply symbolize Julia's revolt against the Party; they are physical things, as Julia's revolt is physical. The Party at least theoretically denies luxuries, for they weaken the commitment of Party members.

The song: "Oranges and Lemons, say the bells of St. Clement's": This, too, like the paperweight, symbolize the faded past; it is an old nursery **rhyme** describing the sound of the bells of the famous old London churches, which have now either been demolished or been turned into war museums. It, too, will recur.

PART TWO: SECTION FIVE

Julia and Winston continue their clandestine meetings in the room above Mr. Charrington's shop. They talk of various things they might do: disappear, adopt Prole accent, live hidden from the Party. Or they might find Goldstein and the Brotherhood and join them to overthrow the Party. Or they might commit suicide. Only this last solution is feasible, because they know that they will be found out no matter what else they do, such is the Party's conditioning and such is its power. Syme, the editor of the *Eleventh Newspeak Dictionary*, "disappears" in this section, as Winston had predicted he would; he is an "unperson."

Comment

This rather long section represents the further development of Winston's revolt, and further points out the differences intellectually and ideologically between Winston and Julia. She regards the "war" in which the Party is perpetually embroiled as a sham, and in this she is far more perceptive than Winston. Winston thinks of Julia and himself as resembling the bit of coral enclosed in the glass paperweight; he imagines that the furnished room is akin to the glass, and that no harm can come to them as long as they maintain this oasis of sanity in the world of the Party. As it will turn out, he is wrong even in this belief.

PART TWO: SECTION SIX

O'Brien makes an excuse to speak with Winston at work, and refers to the Tenth Newspeak Dictionary and to Winston's friend, Syme, the dictionary editor and enthusiast about Newspeak, although he does not mention Syme directly by name. But Syme is more than dead; he is an "unperson." O'Brien must know this. Therefore, what he has said to Winston is, in effect, that he is a conspirator; further, he invites Winston to visit him at home, on a pretext involving the Dictionary. Winston is sure that O'Brien is a representative of the Brotherhood, and he also knows that sooner or later he will obey this summons to meet O'Brien.

Comment

The fear and the **dehumanization** of life in *1984* are further illustrated by the fact that it is very difficult even to find out where people live, unless they tell one directly, as O'Brien does Winston. There are no directories; everyone is, so to speak, anonymous. O'Brien is very careful, as he writes his address on a piece of paper, to give it to Winston right under a telescreen so that the address may be read. But giving his address is not necessarily criminal; mentioning Syme is because of his status in the Party limbo of those who have been vaporized. Winston thus knows the jeopardy in which he is placed; he feels as if he is stepping down into his own grave, even though he had anticipated this. As he had written at the beginning of his revolt: "Thoughtcrime does not entail death: Thoughtcrime is death." Now he knows that he is coming closer to his own downfall and vaporization.

PART TWO: SECTION SEVEN

This section begins with another of Winston's dreams, in which his heretofore repressed belief that he had "murdered" his mother spills over into his conscious mind. It ends with Winston and Julia discussing how, if at all, it is impossible to keep from the kind of selfishness and corruption by the Party symbolized by the dream.

Comment

The corruption of the individual by the Party is nowhere better illustrated in Part Two than in the dream or fantasy about his childhood which Winston undergoes at this point. The chocolate incident, in which Winston remembers snatching a bit of chocolate from his starving baby sister aged two or three, is unbearably pathetic, and had obviously scarred him with deep guilt feelings. Winston's mother, he realizes now, had been sure that she would "disappear" just as Winston's father had disappeared. But she did not tell him; what good would telling him have done? Winston believes that he had killed his mother in some way by taking the chocolate; of course this is pure fantasy, but his guilt feelings are the important thing here. In turn, his dream of murdering his mother is related to the earlier dream he had had about seeing his mother and sister sinking deeper and deeper into green sea water. Here Julia, who reassures him, and Winston conclude that the only way you can beat "them" is by feeling that one must stay human - this is related to the important point that Winston has that the Proles are human because they still have regard for human feelings, while he, Julia, and the Party have lost their humanity, and at best can provide a basis for a humanization sometime in the future.

PART TWO: SECTION EIGHT

Winston and Julia visit O'Brien in his private apartment where, as a member of the Inner Party, he has the privilege of turning off his telescreen, as he tells them. Actually, as will be made clear later, this is a trap, and everything Winston and Julia say is recorded and they are photographed. O'Brien offers a toast to his "Leader" - the leader of the Brotherhood, Emmanuel Goldstein,. He tells them of the work of the Brotherhood, and says that he will provide Winston with a copy of the Book: Goldstein's books that outlines the present system of society and how to change it. Julia and Winston swear loyalty to the Brotherhood and vow that what they learn of it will remain secret even under torture.

Comment

An elaborate deception is staged here for Winston and Julia. Though they do not know it, this is evidently the culmination of a long-standing plot against them by the Party. Winston, especially, has been watched for years, as it appears from the pattern of incidents in his life, the dreams he has had (perhaps involving hypnotic suggestion by the Party), and the way in which O'Brien has taken an interest in him. Probably Winston was under suspicion ever since his father and mother were arrested and no doubt vaporized.

O'Brien greets him with grave courtesy. He offers the pair some wine, which is generally a luxury forbidden to any who are not in the Inner Party. He asks Winston and Julia if they are prepared to commit acts of murder, sabotage, treason, forgery, blackmail, and indeed anything at all the Brotherhood orders.

They agree; this, too, will be used against them by the Thought Police to show that they are not even ethically superior to the Party, because they have agreed to use the same methods as the Party uses in order to attain and maintain power. All that Winston and Julia can accomplish with their revolt is to effect a change at some indefinite time in the future; this is all that O'Brien promises them. Winston significantly drinks a toast to "the past"; this should be considered symbolically in the light of the Party slogan, "... who controls the Past controls the Future." Also, it should be remembered that Winston's work in the Ministry of Truth consists of systematically falsifying the Past "We shall meet again . . . in the place where there is no darkness," O'Brien gravely repeats to Winston. They both recognize the **allusion**; probably the phrase has been repeated to Winston by Party agents or psychologists while he has slept. As the section is concluded, Winston is looking forward to receiving the Book which will tell him "why" - why the world is the way it is, and what he can do to change it.

PART TWO, SECTION NINE

In this section, Winston's enlightenment begins. He receives the Book, and begins to read it in Mr. Charrington's room above the shop. It is *The Theory and Practice of Oligarchical Collectivism*, by Emmanuel Goldstein. The portions of the Book which Winston reads, part aloud to Julia, are vitally important in understanding Orwell's conception of the society of *1984* and his technique of projecting tendencies of the present into the future. While it may be dull reading, it provides a key; rightly understood, the ideas contained in it are literally dynamite.

Comment

"The essence of oligarchical rule is not father-to-son inheritance, but the persistence of certain world-view and a certain way of life, imposed by the dead upon the living." This is one of the key descriptions of what Goldstein's Book calls "the theory and practice of oligarchical collectivism." The Party's object is to nominate its successors and thereby remain in power forever. The theory of the Party is analyzed separately in an essay below in connection with a discussion of Orwell's views on James Burnham's *The Managerial Revolution*. But one point which has not been made sufficiently clear in previous analyses of *1984* is that there is "hidden evidence" throughout Parts One and Two suggesting that Winston has been the victim of a fiendishly elaborate long-term plot by the Party-in which he would be tempted and entrapped into Thoughtcrime so that he would provide one more example and opportunity for the exercise of naked power which the Party desires for its own sake, as is explained in Goldstein's book-which was almost certainly written by a member or members of the Inner Party - and as O'Brien explains the Party's objectives to Winston in Part Three.

PART TWO: SECTION TEN

In this final section, Winston, having been enlightened to the point where part of his question, the "why" of the Party, is answered, apparently sleeps around the clock in his cheap furnished room, with Julia by his side. Without having finished the Book, he knows that Goldstein's final message must be that if there is hope, it must be in the Proles. But in the very moment when he reaches even this level of enlightenment, he and Julia are arrested, in their room, by the Thought Police, and Mr. Charrington, whose disguise has been removed, turns out to have been an agent of the Thought Police.

Comment

Obviously, the Party has gone to fantastic lengths to trap Winston and Julia. They have been given some insight into the workings of the Party, only to make the downfall more painful to them. The hidden room of Mr. Charrington turns out to have been as private as a fishbowl, with a telescreen behind a picture and Mr. Charrington, a highly trained and quite professional agent of the Thought Police, apparently devoting all of his time just to Winston's case. For Winston is clearly the person the Party is after; Julia is not nearly as important to the Party, because her revolt is not intellectual or ideological, but largely physical. For good reason, then, Winston is more dangerous to the Party. As Part Two ends, the glass paper weight with the bit of pink coral is callously shattered to pieces by a policeman; this symbolizes the breaking of the charmed circle - the end of the temporarily separate and secure existence, safe in their own ideas of each other, of Winston and Julia.

PART TWO: SUMMARY

In Part Two, Winston briefly discovers the Golden Country which he has dreamed of in Part One. In the discussion of Orwell's lesser-known novel, *Coming Up for Air*, this never-never land, this Golden Country, is much in the thoughts of the **protagonist**, George Bowling, who is himself (somewhat like Winston Smith) representative of "the common man" while simultaneously being a most uncommon man in the depth of his social perceptions But George Bowling's mind is often on the times before the War (the First World War, that is), when he was a boy growing up. For him, the Golden Country includes a hidden pool of large fish set in a rural scene; a place George had visited as a boy and was always looking to return to. But when he finally finds the pool, and this as a rather chubby red-faced man of forty-five with two children, a shrewish wife, and a salesman's job which he neither likes nor hates, the Golden Country is changed. In fact, it is no more; the pool is there, but the fish have gone, and the trees have been chopped down, and old rusty pieces of junked automobiles, tin cans, and worn-out tires have been thrown into the pool to pollute it thoroughly. "You can't go home again," George Bowling finds-you can't return to Lower Binfield, his boyhood home before the War, and find it as it was. The state of innocence, relatively speaking, before 1914, in Orwell's reading of history, has been succeeded by a state of corrupt experience and by the "streamlined men from Eastern Europe," who think in slogans and speak in bullets, and whose means of persuasion are the machine gun, the rubber truncheon, and the concentration camp. George Bowling's experience is, on a different, more allegorical level, Winston Smith's.

Another symbol in Part Two is the glass paperweight. Winston and Julia are temporarily insulated from the grim reality of the Party's world, just as if they were preserved under glass.. The smashing of the paperweight signals the end of their dream of escape.

It is essential to the Party's plan for Winston that he should not be arrested until he has read the Book by Goldstein. He must understand what is being done to him, and why. If the suggestion is not too bizarre (of course, everything in Winston's world is bizarre), it may be observed that Winston's reading of the Book is like a student's preparation for a series of classes by the reading of an assigned textbook. The Book is almost certainly, as has been said, a product of the Party itself; the Brotherhood and Goldstein probably do not exist, except as artificial creations of the Party.

The classes for which Winston is preparing, however, are no ordinary classes. His College will be the Ministry of Truth, his classrooms will be the rooms in the subbasement from which few or none emerge really alive, his teacher will be O'Brien, and the method of instruction will be argumentation and the dialectical process validated by torture and by sheer physical force. This is to be the content of Part Three: the re-education of Winston Smith not in objective truth but in Party truth.

1984

TEXTUAL ANALYSIS

PART THREE

....

PART THREE: SECTION ONE

With his arrest, Winston's ordeal by fire begins-his descent into the underworld both literally (the cellars of the Ministry of Love) and figuratively. All the techniques of an advanced and fiendish investigative police science are used to break Winston down and make him into what the Party desires him to be. The cramped, smelly surroundings in the cells are the preliminary part of the treatment for brainwashing political prisoners, as is the interminable waiting under the gaze of the telescreens which Winston undergoes. When O'Brien enters the cell, escorted by a brute of a guard, Winston at first believes that O'Brien, too, is under arrest. But he is not; he is one of those directing the entire treatment of Winston. "You knew this, Winston . . . don't deceive yourself. You did know it-you have always known it." Yes, Winston told himself, he had known that O'Brien was not what he seemed

Comment

Winston had at least on the subconscious level known that O'Brien was not an agent of the Brotherhood, and that sooner or later the trap would close. Orwell provides a hint of a psychological explanation of the relationship between O'Brien and Winston, which is curiously ambivalent; they should be mortal enemies, but in a curious way respect and even like each other, though Winston realizes that in terms of sheer intellectual capacity O'Brien is clearly his superior. But if Winston knew that his relationship with O'Brien would result in his entrapment, why did he go ahead with it and seek to join the Brotherhood, imperiling not only himself but also Julia? The answer Orwell provides seems a twofold one. In the first place, Winston is seeking not so much to be loved or liked as simply to be understood-to communicate with even one human being who will understand how he feels and why he believes it to be so important that two plus two equal four. O'Brien understands him; they both know this. As a trusted and dedicated member of the Inner Party, O'Brien can yet be objective about Winston's act of Thoughtcrime, and Winston is grateful for this objectivity.

A second suggestion as to why Winston enters the trap has to do with his feelings of guilt, as expressed in several of the dreams previously discussed. Winston feels guilty over his real or imagined treatment of his mother and sister as a child; he also has the feeling that he is guilty for allowing himself to be made no longer human by the Party. Recent psychology and criminology have assumed, on the basis of abundant evidence, that often when one has transgressed a law it is because he is seeking to be punished, on the unconscious level at any rate. And it is fairly clear-although Orwell does not spell this out but instead lets Winston's thoughts and actions speak for themselves - that Winston is seeking punishment for his fancied guilt. His guilt feelings actually stem from the fact that before he undergoes his brainwashing in the cellars of the Ministry of Love he is still human, despite his saying to Julia that only the Proles are still human in *1984*. He feels guilty for being what he is.

Julia hardly appears at all in Part Three, except for a meeting with Winston right at the end which shows how completely the Party has changed the two of them. Julia never really understood Winston; their relationship, although involving a revolt against the Party, had been almost entirely physical. Thus, Julia, intelligent but essentially unreflective, submits quickly and completely to the Thought Police, signs every confession, and apparently undergoes the kind of religious conversion in reverse which the Party desires. Winston's is a more difficult case; it is therefore a paradox that he is best understood not by Julia, but by his long-term tormentor, O'Brien.

The sordid surroundings of the cells to which Winston is taken with their emphasis on physical dirt, may have some suggestion of Orwell's picture of the "W.C. and dirty-handkerchief side of life" in the essay "Such, Such Were the Joys..." But it is more likely that, as Swift did in *Gulliver's Travels*, he was symbolizing moral corruption by physical nastiness, to show the degeneration of society.

PART THREE: SECTION TWO

Winston undergoes a preliminary series of physical and mental tortures at this point in his imprisonment, the purpose of which is to soften him up. For the Party goes not merely wish him to confess to the commission of almost every imaginable crime - this is but the beginning of his treatment. The beatings, the starvation, the psychological pressure, all dislocate Winston's sense of reality still further. And when he is judged to be ready, he is placed under the special personal care of O'Brien who, as he holds such a high position in the Inner Party, would normally not concern himself with an Outer Party Thoughtcriminal such as Winston.

Comment

This is an important section, because it begins the bizarre dialogue between Winston and O'Brien which will occupy much of the third and final Part of *1984,* leading to Winston's reformation and re-education in Party discipline and logic. At first Winston undergoes a preliminary routine interrogation, which apparently is a matter of course in such cases. He confesses to a long range of crimes: sabotage, espionage, while being beaten with steel rods, whips, and rubber truncheons. After the physical comes the mental; not brutal guards but Party intellectuals, who question him in relays under glaring lights, and keep him in slight physical discomfort, but do not actually beat him. They were worse, he finds, than those who beat him physically; they break him down further. He confesses that he murdered his wife, even though both he and his torturers know that she is still alive; he confesses to being a religious believer, an admirer of capitalism, and a sexual pervert. In a strange way, these lies are true. By committing Thoughtcrime he had willed all these acts, and for the Party, thoughts and inclinations are more important than overt action, because the Party must have adherents who think only thoughts which it approves. The thought is prior to the act, in contrast with conventional Anglo-Saxon concepts of justice and law which regard only acts. (See the discussion of "The Law in *1984,*" above.)

This section provides a graphic account of a perfected system of brainwashing, originally pioneered by the totalitarian states of the 1930s and 1940s. It is quite realistic; Orwell was simply projecting a bit ahead to see what brainwashing and thought control might be like if the power using these techniques had assigned such things as a chief subject of long-term scientific investigation. All that the Party has done along these lines has not fully satisfied it; what is still desired is a way to read the thoughts of a human being at any time against his will. Orwell implies that this objective, too, will ultimately be realized by the Party.

Winston had felt that all along O'Brien was watching over his treatment. In his dreams O'Brien appears, along with a shadowy concept, "Room 101." We shall learn subsequently what is in Room 101; it is the worst thing in the world, but different for each person. "I shall save you, I shall make you perfect," O'Brien has told Winston in his dreams. Indeed, O'Brien admits that he has watched over Winston for seven years, in preparation for this culminating action. But why should the Party spend so much time with one minor Thoughtcriminal?

Winston finds the answer to this and other questions from O'Brien. In this section there begins a Socratic dialogue, new style; in fact, Orwell may well have gotten the idea for the confrontation between O'Brien and Winston Smith from the dialogues of Plato - *The Republic*, for example. But the dialogue situation now is different - O'Brien speaks with Winston while holding in his hand a dial controlling a torture machine which can inflict pain to any degree desired on Winston. This is the ultimate in torture; instead of the free exchange of ideas, there is complete physical subjection of one participant in the dialogue to the other.

PART THREE: SECTION THREE

O'Brien anticipates some of Winston's questions, beginning with why the Ministry of Love should spend so much time and trouble with him. O'Brien explains that he had written, or at any rate collaborated in writing, the Book by Emmanuel Goldstein. He describes the program for overthrowing the Party set forth in it as nonsense; the Proles will never revolt until they become conscious, and will never become conscious. He asks Winston why the Party does what it does. Winston answers that the Party acts because it desires to bring about the good of mankind, who are incapable of ruling themselves. But O'Brien tortures him further, saying that the Party desires power solely for its own sake. The object of power is power. Power in the Party's sense can even triumph over the inevitable death of the individual, because the Party is immortal even if the individual is not.

Comment

O'Brien tells Winston that in his education there are three stages: learning, understanding, and acceptance. Section Two of Part Three deals with Winston's learning what the Party and the system really are. Section Three is the stage of understanding, while Sections Four and Five are the stages of acceptance, wherein Winston will become what the Party desires, totally and forever. "If you want a picture of the future, imagine a boot stamping on a human face-forever." These words, spoken by O'Brien to Winston Smith in the torture chamber, are among the most famous in *1984*. Orwell once wrote, in his essay "England, Your England" (1941), that the goose step is one of the most horrible sights in the world, far more terrifying than a dive bomber. "It is simply an affirmation of naked power," he wrote; "contained in it, quite consciously and intentionally, is the vision of a boot crashing down on a face." One of the essential differences between totalitarianism and a republican or democratic form of government is that under totalitarianism there is no law, there is only power and the exertion of power, often against the helpless. The naked power exerted by the Party in *1984* is only an extension of the kind of power desired by, say, Nazi and Fascist governments, in Orwell's view. But even the Nazis claimed that the end of power would be to create a "better world," in which a Master Race would rule over all other races and, presumably, war would no longer occur.

But in Orwell's projection of this power madness, the governments of the future will not deceive themselves as to their intentions. They do not wish to save the world; they wish only to maintain themselves in power, indefinitely and with no outside interference. Hence the tacit agreements, completely unwritten and even unspoken, between Oceania, Eurasia, and Eastasia, to fight perpetual but limited wars whose purpose is not conquest but rather economic equilibrium. War being thus converted into Peace, each state can turn its attention to its own citizens, who will provide limitless opportunities for the exertion of power against them, as Winston is here doing.

Winston cannot answer O'Brien; he feels that something will defeat the Party. Life, the Spirit of Man, Human Nature, even God - not that Winston is a religious believer - will prevent the Party from realizing its (to him) insane objectives. Winston considers himself morally superior to the Party. But O'Brien breaks him down still further by showing him a mirror image of himself. Winston is a physical wreck, emaciated, literally rotting away. He breaks down in tears when he sees what "they" have done to him; O'Brien's answer is that he did this to himself, by setting up his will against that of the Party. There is but one thing left to Winston that permits him to hold on to his integrity, or at least a shred of it: he has not betrayed Julia. He has continued to love her. And he feels grateful to O'Brien that O'Brien at least understands this. In the end, Winston knows, he will be shot, but first his cure must be completed.

PART THREE: SECTION FOUR

Winston has already been broken by the Party; in this section, we see him training himself in the techniques of Crimestop, which is the antidote to Thoughtcrime. Two and Two make Five, he writes; this is what he has learned under the tortures of O'Brien. If the Party says that a thing is so, it is so. But Winston has still not betrayed Julia, who is the one person in the world whom he still loves. Further, he hates Big Brother, the embodiment of the Party. Therefore, O'Brien comes for him in the night to conduct him to Room 101 for the final stage of his treatment.

Comment

As Winston's education proceeds, he has learned and understood the system, but he has not yet accepted it on the deepest level. In his unconscious, often expressed through his dreams, there still exists the Golden Country and also Julia. The Party allows him to recover his physical health somewhat; he is well fed and not tormented any longer by his torturers. The Party must be right, he concludes. Further, he must have been wrong to set his will up against Big Brother. Sanity is statistical, the Party teaches; there is no objective right and wrong; all is relative. Winston is prepared to believe this, too, in defiance of logic.

But one night, while dreaming of the Golden Country, Winston cries out in his sleep: "Julia! Julia! Julia! my love! Julia!"

He has betrayed himself again; deep down, he is still a rebel, for there is one human being whom he values still more than the Party and Big Brother. Quite soon, O'Brien appears at the door of his cell, with a secret police officer and guards. "Room 101," O'Brien says, motioning towards Winston. It is not enough to obey Big Brother; Winston must now love him. The treatment in Room 101, whatever it is, will ensure this.

PART THREE: SECTION FIVE

In Room 101, as O'Brien has said before, is the worst thing in the world. The room itself is far underground; it is, in fact, a hell where those who have sinned against the Party undergo their final punishment. The torture to be inflicted on Winston consists of a cage attached to a face mask. In the cage are starving rats. If the door of the cage is opened while the prisoner is wearing the mask, the rats will attack the victim's face. O'Brien lectures to Winston on the history of this torture, telling him that in his case the worst thing in the world happens to be rats. He, Winston, will do what is required; O'Brien will not tell him what this is as he adjusts the mask. "Do it to Julia! Not me! Julia!" Winston screams, as the mask clicks shut rather than open, preventing the rats from attacking him.

Comment

This grotesque scene represents the **climax** of Winston's treatment. It is obvious that the Party and its spies and secret policemen have for years studied everything about Winston. And, as O'Brien tells him, everyone has something which represents an absolutely unreasoning fear. In Winston's case it is rats, as the Party spies have found out. But O'Brien, while tormenting him with the description of what the rats will do to him once the mask of the cage is opened, will not tell Winston what is expected of him.

What is expected, in this short and brutal exchange between torturer and victim, is that Winston will interpose his beloved, Julia, between himself and the rats. "I don't care what you do to her. Tear her face off, strip her to the bones. Not me! Julia! Not me!"

This heralds Winston's complete downfall. The Party has now broken him forever. The one thing he has loved he has, at least symbolically, killed, and he is merely a shell of a man now. Winston has indeed been emptied of himself and filled with the thoughts and, even more important, with the feelings and emotions appropriate to a good Party member who loves Big Brother.

PART THREE: SECTION SIX

After Winston is broken by the torture in Room 101, he is no longer dangerous to the Party; in fact, the Party would prefer him to be able to walk around free as another living testimony to its exercise of power. He is released and given a sinecure job in the company of similar shells of men. Winston visits the Chestnut Tree cafe and drinks Victory (synthetic) gin, just as he had seen the confessed enemies of the Party, Jones, Aaronson, and Rutherford do this earlier. Winston even meets Julia, but whatever love or affection had been between them is dead; they view each other with horror, confessing that each had betrayed the other. When they separate, it is with no desire to see each other again. In the midst of the announcement over the telescreen of a great victory over Eurasia, Winston, gazing at the enormous and powerful face of Big Brother, in that moment has won the victory over himself, and loves Big Brother.

Comment

The ending of the book may appear ambiguous in that Winston apparently continues to live. "In the end we will shoot you," O'Brien has told him. But one never knows the time of the execution, except that the Party cannot afford to execute rebels until they have been reformed, as Winston has been. Actually, it is not important whether Winston is actually shot at the end of the book. He dreams that he is about to be shot, his reformation being now complete. But the important thing is that his fate no longer matters: he is among the walking dead. Every human feeling has been taken from him, as it has from Julia. The Party is no longer interested in them; Winston is hardly watched any longer. Though he has a make-work job on an "Interim Committee" at better pay than he had ever enjoyed before, and with light or no duties, he actually serves another, more important function in society. By his very existence as a reformed Thoughtcriminal, Winston Smith provides the Party with the endless self-congratulation it needs at its successful use of its overwhelming power against a dissenter.

The "yellow note" on the telescreen in the Chestnut Tree cafe is symbolic of the Party's victory. "Under the spreading chestnut tree I sold you and you sold me - " the telescreen says to Winston, as it had said to Jones, Aaronson, and Rutherford. It is a constant reminder that all of them had been broken; it makes them aware of their fate. They know that they are victims, but can do nothing about it. Always the victims of the Party will exist as a group, though individuals will die, because it is necessary for the Party to have victims whom it can dominate and destroy, as it has dominated and destroyed Winston Smith.

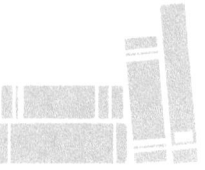

1984

APPENDIX

THE PRINCIPLES OF NEWSPEAK AND "POLITICS AND THE ENGLISH LANGUAGE"

The linguistic **satire** of *1984* in part stems from, or at any rate parallels, a similar kind of **satire** in several works of a writer whom Orwell very much admired: Jonathan Swift. In Swift's *A Tale of a Tub*, and in Book III of *Gulliver's Travels*, there is a brilliant **satire** on what Swift considered to be the corruption of language for political or religious purposes. Swift's ideal of expression involved, above all things , clearness and precision of meaning. As he said in *A Tale of a Tub*, a **satire** on religious controversy and on the difference between true and sham religion, if a work really contains "light," that is, if it really is clear and has something to say, this fact will be apparent immediately to the average reader, who does not need extraordinary intelligence or perceptiveness to comprehend the truth, if the truth is in fact present. On the other hand, if it is the purpose of the writer deliberately to conceal his meaning and to confuse, he may do this under a fog of inexact, ill-chosen, and imprecise words. For Swift, this is a perversion of language.

So with Orwell: for him, much political writing seeks not to reveal the truth, but to conceal it. The corruption of the English Language, which for Orwell was at its best a precise and noble medium of expression, takes two forms. The first, in *1984*, involved the limitation of meaning and thought; as he put, in the Appendix to *1984*, "The purpose of Newspeak was not only to provide a medium of expression for the world-view and mental habits proper to the devotee of Ingsoc, but to make all other modes of thought impossible."

This is an apparent impossibility, but it can be brought about by narrowing or destroying the **connotations** of words, so that each word will have one, and only one, meaning. Orwell, of course, exaggerates for the purposes of his **satire**. Allied with this stripping away of **connotations** (secondary meanings of words, as opposed to denotations, or primary meanings) is the process which he described in his essay "Politics and the English Language," published in 1946 just as he was seriously thinking about the subject matter of *1984*. This process involves the decline of a language through political and economic causes, leading to deliberate lack of precision and use of soothing euphemisms as a substitute for hard reality. Thus political opponents of a totalitarian regime are not murdered or shot, they are eliminated or liquidated: words which do not carry the same **connotations** of brutality and tend therefore to obscure what is really happening. Stale words or neutral euphemisms become a substitute for thought. Both processes-narrowing of **connotation** and use of neutral euphemisms-are illustrated in *1984*. Thus, "Politics and the English Language" is highly recommended for reading with the Appendix to *1984*.

Newspeak is a sort of exaggeration of Basic English, but the intent of the Party in making Newspeak the official language of

Oceania has not involved the wish to simplify or the wish to make the language easier to learn by limiting the number of words and word relationships. Rather, the intent is obscurantist: to make certain thoughts impossible by removing the very concept in which these thoughts might be phrased from the English language. Thus, even a dictionary becomes a political document; the dictionary on which Syme is working, the *Eleventh Newspeak Dictionary*, is part of a gradual narrowing down of the meanings of words to prevent political heresy. "Free," for example, in Newspeak can have no reference to political freedom; it can be used only in a sense such as "the field is free from weeds." Political freedom no longer has even a name. Thus Newspeak diminishes the range of thought.

By the timetable of the Party, Oldspeak, or Standard English as spoken, say, in the 1950s, will have been abolished by the year 2050. The actual language in *1984* is a cross between Newspeak and Oldspeak, as the process of changing language must by its very nature proceed slowly. But Orwell, as he projects ahead, leaves no doubt that given the conditions of life under Big Brother in Oceania, the change will be accomplished on schedule. Newspeak contains three vocabularies, called the A, B, and C vocabularies. The A vocabulary consists of words used in everyday life: what a traveler might need to get along in a foreign country-words involving such processes as eating, drinking, working, cooking, etc. All ambiguities and shades of meaning have been removed from these words, which were fairly neutral in political significance to begin with. It would be impossible to use the A vocabulary for political discussion.

The B vocabulary consists of words which have been constructed for political purposes; these are compound words which are intended to foster approved modes of thought. Thus the word goodthink refers to the duty "to think in an orthodox manner," if one regards it as a verb. Its noun-verb is goodthink; its past tense and past participle is goodthinked; its present participle is goodthinking; its adjective is goodthinkful; its adverb, goodthinkwise; its verbal noun, goodthinker.

These are abstract political concepts, but rigidly limited in meaning. They tend to reduce even the possibility of Thoughtcrime, while on the other hand, abstract words such as honor, justice, morality, internationalism, democracy, science, and religion have ceased to exist. These are, for the Party, dangerous words which may at least increase the possibility of Thoughtcrime. Many of the words in the B vocabulary were euphemisms, similar to those of which Orwell wrote earlier in "Politics and the English Language." Minipax is a contraction for Ministry of Peace, which is concerned with War. Joycamp is a euphemism for "forced labor camp" or "concentration camp"; Orwell perhaps got this satiric idea from certain euphemisms used to describe Nazi concentration camps, over the entrance to one of which was inscribed the cynical motto, so close to the thought of the Party in *1984:* Arbeit Macht Frei ("work will make you free").

The C vocabulary is a specialized scientific and technical vocabulary, but the ordinary citizen of *1984* would have little need for these words, and would not be encouraged to learn them.

In practice, heretical thoughts, then, are hardly possible. By 2050, the Party believes, they will be completely impossible. One might say "All men are equal," but the meaning would be limited to the sense in which one might say, "All men are redhaired." The secondary meaning, or **connotation**, of legal or political equality would have been purged from the word "equal." One could say, "Big Brother is ungood," but by the time of the establishment of a complete Newspeak vocabulary, the statement would merely convey in meaning a self-evident absurdity.

Great literature is, for Orwell, an affirmation of man's liberty. Thus, the Party was engaged either in suppressing it, or in translating such literature into Newspeak: Shakespeare, Milton, Swift, Byron, and Dickens were to be translated, and when the task was complete, sometime around 2050, the original writings of these men would be destroyed, because the words which they used might tend to promote heretical thoughts in their readers.

"Political language," wrote Orwell in "Politics and the English Language," "is designed to make lies sound truthful and murder respectable, and to give the appearance of solidity to pure wind." The process which he saw as beginning in the 1930s and 1940s of the corruption of the English language had developed, from the point of view of his satiric purpose, by 1984 into Newspeak. Yet Orwell thought of the process as subject to being reversed, as he wrote in this same essay. This is a hopeful sign, and tends to support the view, expressed earlier herein, that Orwell was not writing a prediction of things to come in *1984,* but rather a warning, so that men would exercise the eternal vigilance which is the price of liberty.

1984

CHARACTER ANALYSES

Because of the satirical purpose which Orwell had in writing *1984*, the characters in the book tend to be shadowy or two-dimensional stereotypes. Thus, only one character in the entire work is presented as a complete and believable human being; that is, of course, Winston Smith. Indeed, Winston is the only human character whose full name is given.

Winston Smith

He is both Everyman, as symbolized by the most common English name, Smith, and the unusual man in his society, as witness the name Winston, which is the name of the man generally thought to have been the greatest Englishman of our age. There is an implied ironic contrast between Winston's first name and his last name, as though the heirs to the great tradition of Winston Churchill, the indomitable wartime Prime Minister of England, have been metamorphosed into frightened robots or sub-men who live in fear not only of their Government but even of their own children, who may denounce them to the Thought Police.

Winston is a frail figure of a man, thirty-nine years old and suffering from a varicose ulcer on his ankle. He is not well nourished, though as a member of the Outer Party, the auxiliary to the ruling class, the elite Inner Party, Winston should have special privileges. But in the society of *1984,* the special privileges of members like Winston seem to consist of the right to be watched for the slightest departure from political orthodoxy. Winston's fate is the book. We see Winston going to his ordinary day's work, which is by any rational standards, but not by the standards of a totalitarian state, sheer lunacy, and we see Winston's revolt, his fall, and his "reformation" ending in his death, literal or figurative.

One of the most important aids to the understanding of the character and motivation of Winston Smith is the series of dreams which he has throughout the book, involving his mother and sister, O'Brien, Julia, "the place where there is no darkness," and the Golden Country. These may be considered in the light of elementary psychological theory, and Orwell quite probably so intended them to be considered-to provide a key to the state of Winston's unconscious or subconscious mind, under the repressions imposed upon him by the Party.

Julia

Julia is Winston's mistress. We never learn her last name, but her name might just as well be Woman as anything more specific. There is a hint of antifeminism in Orwell's characterization of Julia; the women, beginning with Julia (who is herself a rebel against the system), seem less horrified by the brutality of the Party's policies and less concerned with ideology. At any rate, Julia, as a character, is not placed on the same plane as Winston. Her lack of a last name suggests this two-dimensional characterization. Julia's rebellion against the Party is physical only; she has no interest in what Winston learns of the intellectual basis of the system, which is another way of saying that though she is intelligent, Julia is no intellectual. Part of the discrepancy between Julia and Winston may involve simply their respective ages: she is only twenty-six. For Julia, the good is not necessarily freedom, it is physical pleasure, though of course in becoming Winston's mistress she is taking a great risk, as adultery between Party members is severely punished. Julia's downfall might have been predicted; when she is arrested by the Thought Police she immediately confesses everything, and was really a textbook case of torture and reformation. She has no inner strength and no understanding of politics and ideology, so that once the Party seizes her as a rebel it can easily break her to its will.

O'Brien

Again, like Julia, known only by one name. He is a powerfully built man of about forty-five, an intellectual and a member of the Inner Party doing a job in the Ministry of Truth which is very important but is never identified or given a title. Probably O'Brien is one of the collective ruling oligarchies of Oceania. He has been one of the writers of the Book;-Goldstein's *The Theory and Practice of Oligarchical Collectivism*, which is the key to the way Oceania is actually ruled, - and he seems in a hidden way to be used to planning great activities. Apparently Winston is one of his projects, for O'Brien has studied and watched over him for seven years, prior to the opening of the action of *1984*. What is so destructive to Winston Smith is the realization that O'Brien is much more intelligent than Winston himself; his mind comprehends Winston's mind. Yet even as O'Brien is more intelligent, he is also more fanatical and more prepared to accept everything the Party teaches. In fact, he does not merely believe in the system; he is the system. O'Brien is frightening precisely because, being so intelligent, he can by the principles of Doublethink accept the Party's absurd account of what constitutes reality.

Big Brother

He is a man of about forty-five, "with a heavy black moustache and ruggedly handsome features." Rather, he is a picture of a man, and a point of focus for the emotions aroused by Party propaganda. Probably Big Brother does not exist, but when Winston, in the cellars of the Ministry of Love, asks his torturer O'Brien whether Big Brother exists, the answer he receives is: "You do not exist." Winston has been placed outside the stream of history; though he has an objective existence, he is to become an "unperson" and to be vaporized. On the other hand, Big Brother may not exist except in posters and pictures and in the minds of the people, but he is all-powerful just the same, as an embodiment of the power of the Party. The title of the Book, with its suggestion that 1984 is governed by an oligarchical collectivism, is a hint that Big Brother is simply a necessary figurehead. Several commentators on *1984* have suggested that Big Brother is representative of Stalin, but Orwell's **satire** was far more universal than simply an attack on Stalinism.

Emmanuel Goldstein

The "Enemy of the People" and the converse of Big Brother. He is probably a creation of the Party also, and serves as a focus for the hatred generated by the Party against enemies, whether real or imagined, whom the Party can blame for whatever shortages, bombings, and other occurrences are suffered by the people of

Oceania. He appears on the telescreens during the Two Minutes Hate. As Big Brother at least suggests Stalin, so Goldstein suggests a leader of the Russian Revolution whom Stalin subsequently disgraced and had assassinated: Leon Trotsky. The fact of Goldstein's Jewish name, alluded to by Orwell, in no way indicates that Orwell was being anti-Semitic; quite the reverse. For Emmanuel Goldstein, by being "against" Big Brother, represents those who are against the iron system of Oceania. Whether the Brotherhood which he leads really exists, having as its object the overthrow of Big Brother, is never made clear: O'Brien tells Winston Smith that he will never know for certain whether it exists. Orwell leaves this point ambiguous, but the probability is that neither Goldstein nor the Brotherhood exist.

Mr. Charrington

The elderly proprietor of the antique shop, who exists in a rundown section of London inhabited mainly by Proles, and who sells Winston Smith a diary and a glass paperweight, and rents him the furnished room which Winston and Julia use as their secret hiding place. Charrington seems an urbane man who lives in the past: a widower aged sixty-two or sixty-three. But at the end of the second Part of *1984*, upon the arrest of Julia and Winston in the furnished room, Charrington's disguise drops away to reveal him with the "cold, alert face of a man of about thirty-five." There has been a telescreen in the room all along, and Charrington is an agent of the Thought Police!

Comrade Ogilvy

A "war hero" of Oceania who allegedly died gloriously at age twenty-three. Actually he is a completely fictitious person who has been invented by Winston Smith in the course of his falsifying of history for the Party. (See discussion in the Analysis and Commentary on Part One: Section Four, above.)

Syme

A little man, an editor of the *Eleventh Newspeak Dictionary*, whom Winston Smith meets at work. While an orthodox member of the Outer Party, there is something not quite right about Syme in Winston's view; he is right, for Syme suddenly disappears; he has become an "unperson." We never learn his first name, and this is true of the other characters.

Mr. And Mrs. Parsons

With their children, Winston's neighbors in Victory Mansions. Mr. Parsons is an enthusiast for all things approved of by the Party, while his wife is a beaten-down, terrified woman, prematurely old. But Parsons is denounced by his own children as a Thoughtcriminal, for saying in his sleep, "Down with Big Brother!" Winston meets Parsons again in "the place where there is no darkness" the cellars of the Ministry of Love.

Ampleforth

A poet, whom Winston also meets in the cellars of the Ministry of Love; he is there for Thoughtcrime, because he had racked his brains for a **rhyme** to the word "rod," and ended up using the word "God," which of course was suspect to the Party.

Jones, Aaronson, And Rutherford

Three men, formerly high up in the Party, who were convicted as traitors, confessed after an elaborate show trial (reminiscent of the Russian purge trials in 1937) were released, re-arrested, and executed as a warning to other prospective traitors and Thoughtcriminals. What is particularly important about them is that after their torture Winston Smith had seen them at the Chestnut Tree Cafe. More to the point, Winston has had in his possession at one time documentary evidence that what the Party had said about them, and their own confessions, were lies. Rightly explained to the people of Oceania, the significance of the evidence Winston has (perhaps unknown to himself with the connivance of the Party, which seeks to entrap Winston still further) could "blow the Party to atoms." But, as O'Brien points out to Winston while torturing him, who would listen? Anyway, it has been Winston who was wrong about the three men, through a failure in Crimestop.

Katharine

Winston Smith's beautiful, but fanatical and brainless wife, whom he considers murdering on one occasion. She does not actually appear in *1984* except as a symbolic presence: symbolic, that is, of what the Party has been able to do to the normal instincts of men and women. Winston and she had only been married fifteen months when they separated, which the Party allowed because there were no children. Katharine is contrasted with Julia, who has managed to remain relatively uncorrupted by the conditioning of the Party, at least until the time of Julia's capture and torture by the Thought Police. Katharine is still alive during the action of *1984*, but as divorce is forbidden by the Party, Winston is technically still married to her.

The Proles

The faceless masses, some 85 per cent of the population of Oceania. The Revolution had allegedly been made for them, but as is explained in Goldstein's *The Theory and Practice of Oligarchical Collectivism*, the lower classes, or Proles, will not benefit from the Revolution at all. Far from establishing, in Marxist terms, "the dictatorship of the Proletariat," and the gradual "withering away of the State," the Revolution has imposed the most extreme form of tyranny on everybody. The Proles are contemptuously dismissed by the Party as subhuman. The Party rather encourages their moral corruption to make them easier to handle. But Winston believes that if there is any hope for the future, it lies in the Proles. O'Brien is at pains to explain to him, as he is being tortured, why this hope is futile: the Proles cannot become self-aware until they revolt, and vice versa.

1984

CRITICAL COMMENTARY

There are relatively few good essays concerning *1984* specifically, and to date there has, at least in the opinion of the author of the present study, been no definitive critical biography or critical study of George Orwell. The material on the relation of James Burnham's *The Managerial Revolution* to *1984* is of major significance, and the reader should consult the note on this subject above.

BIOGRAPHIES

The most elaborate studies of Orwell available, each of which has a chapter on *1984,* are the books by John Atkins, Christopher Hollis, and Richard Rees. The latter two writers were personal acquaintances of George Orwell, and their books contain first hand reminiscences of some value which no doubt will assist in the writing of a definitive study someday. Perhaps we have been too close to Orwell, since his death a decade and a half ago, to have the kind of perspective which leads to a major work of criticism being written about him. So far the criticism is potential, not actual. Yet he is an important writer; perhaps the major English writer of the 1940s and early 1950s, though this is an extreme claim to make. His place in literary history today is by no means settled, and there are good reasons why this should be so. For in considering the ultimate reputation and relative worth of a man of letters, the local and topical is inevitably separated out from that which is more universal, more appealing to all ages and conditions of men. Were *Animal Farm* and *1984* the great successes they were because of the immediacy of their appeal, for they were published just at the point where the full chaos and danger of the postwar world, with its confrontation between former allies of East and West, was becoming clear? Or do these books have a more timeless appeal? Just as Swift's *Gulliver's Travels* contains much local **satire** of English political and religious controversy of the early part of the eighteenth century, so Orwell's writing contains similar material. But what of its universality? This is the question which a critic must answer at some point when dealing with Orwell. Put another way, was Orwell a brilliant but ephemeral journalist, or did the body of his work have more solidity than is represented by even brilliant journalism, which after all, by definition appeals to the moment and not to the long view of history?

Orwell was written about during his lifetime, and John Atkins attempted to summarize some of the views expressed about him in his book, *George Orwell: A Literary and Biographical Study*, which is a rather ambitious work, and this may be consulted. Lionel Trilling, in his well-known essay, "George Orwell and the Politics of Truth," said with economy and restraint what many have said about Orwell: that he was an honest and honorable man as well as an honest man of letters. The entire point of the essay, which Professor Trilling originally wrote as an introduction to *Homage to Catalonia*, may be summed up in the words of one of his students which Trilling himself quotes:

"He [Orwell] was a virtuous man." For Professor Trilling, Orwell was not a genius. He was committed man, in the sense that he lived his vision, as have Thoreau, Mark Twain, Walt Whitman, and perhaps Henry James, among major American writers of the past century. Orwell, in fact, was more modern than these; he was "engaged" in the sense that some of the Existentialists have been engaged and committed to political thought and action for the betterment of human life, whether or not they believed at the time that betterment was possible.

All of Orwell's writing, as Professor Trilling and others have indicated, was directed to political ends which would have as their final result the promotion of human decency. Perhaps there is a lack of really enlightening critical writing about *1984* and other works of Orwell because he was so clear and precise as a writer. Valuing clarity, simplicity, and precision of expression over anything else in the technical craft of writing, Orwell may have said what he had to say in such a forceful way that interpretation was not as necessary as it might be in dealing with more complicated, allegorical, "literary" writers. Sir Richard Rees was a close friend of George Orwell, and it has been said that he is one of the characters, Ravelston, in *Keep the Aspidistra Flying*, though this has not been proved.

It is significant that the title of Sir Richard's book is *George Orwell: Fugitive from the Camp of Victory*. For Orwell, the just man would not be found in the camp of victory, perhaps because in a state of perfect justice (the opposite of *1984,* which is a state of perfect injustice), there would be no camps of strong and weak. Thus, the interpretation of Orwell by Sir Richard involves his always standing up for the weak against the strong, which has occasionally led to the misrepresentation of his real political position.

SPECIAL INTERPRETIVE PROBLEMS

Special problems in the interpretation of *1984* have been dealt with in appropriate sections of this study. But the critical axioms with which the reader should approach Orwell seem reducible to the following: Orwell's biography is very important, as he was above all a writer who lived his work. Second, Orwell's work is a "seamless garment" in which every part of it has a bearing on every other part, and all of his work leads up to *1984* and serves as the best background we have for the interpretation of that great political **satire**. And third, Orwell's purpose in writing was not only to record what was happening in the world and to project ahead in order to make men realize what was likely to happen; it was as much or more his purpose to change the world. He hoped that if he painted political evil vividly enough, men would turn from that evil.

Animal Farm, as a political allegory, of course needs more interpretation than does *1984* in terms of the historical meanings of particular characters and events. The difference between the two best-known and most powerful works of Orwell is that they are not only of different literary kinds - the beast fable and the anti-Utopian fiction - but also *1984* seems to have more universal satirical meanings. Both books deal with what Orwell called "the central question - how to prevent power from being abused." Orwell has no easy answers to this overwhelming question. But he could at least ask it in such a way that his contemporaries could see the absolute importance of the question, and this he did, in language too clear for conventional criticism.

A SELECTION OF VIEWS ON 1984

John Atkins: In his work, *George Orwell* Mr. Atkins correctly assesses all of Orwell's previous work as preparation for *1984*, which book is considered to be Orwell's masterpiece. Mr. Atkins, like Sir Richard Rees and others, attributes the gloom of the ending of *1984* less to ideology than to the fact that Orwell's health had markedly deteriorated as he was writing *1984*.

The point which Atkins makes is that the best analysis of the basis of society in Oceania and indeed the best critique of *1984* may be found in the work itself, in Goldstein's book *The Theory and Practice of Oligarchical Collectivism*. Atkins accepts the thesis of Goldstein's book as one held by Orwell himself: that the end of power is power, that revolutions corrupt those who lead them, that the perpetual state of war which is maintained by the Party is really Peace, as it leads to a sort of bizarre social stability. While much of what Atkins says about *1984* is really summary of the work's contents, the point that Orwell himself believed what he embodied in Goldstein's book as far as politics were concerned is a well-taken one, probably correct. Atkins sees the Party's great secret as its discovery that the sense of reality of most human beings could be dislocated by skillful propaganda, by the process which Orwell called Doublethink.

Atkins also gives examples both from Orwell's previous writing and from contemporary political and social history about the dislocation of reality and the deliberate falsification of the past. Atkins pays especial attention to the Party's debasing of human sexuality in *1984*. Finally Atkins makes what seems to the author of the present study the perfectly valid point that Orwell wrote *1984* not as a prediction of things to come so much as a warning to his contemporaries and immediate successors in Western society that these things - the horrors he described in *1984* - were probabilities if men did not become aware and seek to reverse the trend toward totalitarianism.

Christopher Hollis, in *A Study of George Orwell*, includes a chapter on *1984* which, while it makes essentially the same point as does Atkins about the importance of Goldstein's Book in the understanding of the structure of the work, has a slightly different emphasis than does Atkins. He seems correct in his analysis of Julia's character: she has no **metaphysical** notion of freedom, and no center to her life other than the physical revolt which she engages in with Winston and others-so nothing else can be expected, given her character, than the quick betrayal of Winston which she does under torture. Mr. Hollis also observes that *1984* is not meant as a definite prophecy; Orwell expected and hoped that the book would be a warning so that the society ruled by Big Brother could not come about. Hollis sees that the Party has destroyed virtue and a sense of honor in the men of the society of Oceania, and done its work so well that even if the Party collapsed the system would continue. If the materialism of the Party is true - and Hollis in his interpretation denies that it can be true, on theological and philosophical grounds - then O'Brien is right and Winston Smith is mad: "a flaw in the pattern." O'Brien's premises are thoroughly materialistic. Materialism is a philosophy with a history at least extending back to the pre-Christian, pre-Socratic Greek philosopher, Democritus; thus it is nothing new, and it should be obvious that it can only be opposed on philosophical and religious grounds. This Orwell did, indirectly, in the view of Mr. Hollis; **satire**, of course, is indirect but nevertheless can be effective, as *1984* was enormously effective and influential, at least in alerting people to certain political dangers.

Hollis makes another important point; that *1984* has as one of its chief literary ancestors an anti-Utopia written by a Russian writer, Eugene Zamyatin. The name of Zamyatin's book is *We,* and it was published just after the Second World War. Zamyatin wrote his book in Paris after the Russian Revolution, being disgusted with what he saw as the excesses of the extremists among the Russian revolutionaries, the Bolshevists. *We* purports to be a picture of society as it exists in 2600 A.D. Not only are there parallels between *We* and *1984,* but, as Mr. Hollis points out, Orwell wrote an essay in January, 1946 [See Tribune, January 4, 1946] in which Orwell praised Zamyatin and demonstrated his familiarity with *We*. This was relatively close to the time when he began to compose *1984*. Hollis observes that Orwell was indeed familiar with Zamyatin, but that he adapted the philosophy and world-picture of *We* to the depiction of English society. Hollis ends with a point consistent with the outlook of his book; he, like Orwell, perceives the decay of religious belief and religious values in twentieth-century Western society, but he makes it clear that he does not accept the unreligious or anti-religious attitudes which Orwell in his view seems to have embraced.

Sir Richard Rees sees *Animal Farm* as more obviously a masterpiece than was *1984*. His interpretation of *1984* does not differ in too many particulars from those of Atkins and Hollis, because, as previously observed, the book is so lucid in its **satire** that wide divergence in interpretation is difficult if not impossible. However, Sir Richard has a slightly different view of Julia's character; he does not see it as totally shallow, and he is probably correct in describing her as intelligent but not intellectual. But Julia does not seem a particularly sympathetic character as Orwell drew her; it would be more correct to say that Julia represents life lived only for itself on a physical level which, lacking a philosophy, must fall prey to those who at least hold to some consistent set of beliefs, good or bad.

Sir Richard stresses in his interpretation the ways in which the Party hierarchy is made adoptive and non-hereditary; he also indicates that it was difficult for Orwell to draw characters from the lower classes, in view of his own training and background so that the message of Goldstein's Book, and of Orwell himself: "If there is hope, it lies in the Proles," is not entirely convincing in terms of *1984*. Implied in the interpretation of Rees is the thought that Winston Smith is George Orwell-also a fugitive, ridden by guilt. And this is a valid point. As pointed out in the present study, Winston's dreams are heavily tinged by feelings of guilt, and it may be that the psychological roots of his revolt involve his wishing to be caught, so that his feelings of guilt especially toward his mother may receive their proper punishment.

The idea of Orwell as a "fugitive from the camp of victory" - e.g. from the privileged classes in England, which is advanced by Sir Richard Rees, should be treated with caution; it is by no means the whole explanation of *1984*, and ought not to be taken as such, though it does explain something about the source of many of Orwell's ideas and interests.

Lionel Trilling's well-known essay, "George Orwell and the Politics of Truth," is really part of an introduction to *Homage to Catalonia*, and thus deals with *1984* only indirectly. The suggestion of Professor Trilling is really that Orwell was a very unusual man in his political outlook and in his essential decency-in fact, that he was a sort of modern-day saint, who not only wrote of his vision, but lived it, like Mark Twain, Thoreau, Whitman, Henry Adams, and Henry James.

Orwell was not a genius, said Trilling, but what genius is - the sense in which he used the term, he does not say. He does credit Orwell not only with great imagination and decency, but with a sense of actual participation in the world of affairs so that, unlike many liberal intellectuals in Trilling's view, Orwell knew what he was doing when he wrote of government and administration, of Communism, Nazism, and other political forms. Trilling establishes Orwell's relation to Communism and his disillusion with it - this is also important as one considers what precisely Orwell was satirizing in *1984*. In his final estimation of Orwell as a decent man, and an honest one, Trilling echoes the view held by most who have written about Orwell or known him-indeed, his essay helped to formulate this view.

THE RELATION OF OTHER WORKS OF ORWELL TO 1984

As has been pointed out by at least one critic, everything which Orwell ever wrote was preparation for *1984*. However, in addition to certain essays which have been mentioned in the biographical or the critical commentary sections of this study, two of Orwell's books stand out as worthy of consideration in this context: *Down and Out in Paris and London* (1933), and *Coming up for Air* (1939). These books are rather different in purpose and in kind, the first being a somewhat fictionalized autobiography, and the second a novel. But we will discuss each in turn.

Down and Out in Paris and London was written out of impressions Orwell gained during the period from 1927, when he resigned from the Indian Imperial Police while on leave in England, and 1933, when he re-emerged from the state of deprivation that he had evidently volunteered for. It would take as much closer study of this period of Orwell's life than has previously been done to account for it fully. The most convincing explanation seems to be that Orwell wished at least temporarily to sink to the level of the poor and find out what they were really like and what the quality of their daily life might be. His theory was that very little is known about lower-class life; as he says of the Proles in *1984*, "nobody knew much about the way they lived." Orwell seems to have undergone feelings of guilt at his privileged position as a white sahib in the British Government

Service in Burma, and the guilt feelings may have given rise to a desire to be punished by suffering what the lower classes suffer. But all this is speculation.

Orwell said that everything in this remarkable book actually happened to him, beginning in Paris when he ran out of money, but that he took certain liberties with the order of the events. In the book he describes his work as a Paris plongeur or dish washer, working at least six twelve-hour working days a week (and sometimes seven) in the kitchen of a fashionable Paris hotel, at wages of five hundred francs a month, a mere pittance. The unsatisfying, and indeed stupefying quality of this life, and the reasons why men do such work, undergo close analysis by Orwell. It is a description of the sordid. Still, he has not touched bottom, for he is at least employed and as the hotel provides food and drink free, he is able to live, though he has no time to read, to travel, or to do anything except eat, sleep, drink, and work - the drink being a fortification against the dulling fatigue of such work. "A plongeur is one of the slaves of the modern world," he wrote, and one is utterly convinced of the truth of this statement by the time that the section of the book comes to an end.

Subsequently Orwell does touch bottom, as he quits his job as a dishwasher to work in a highly questionable Paris bistro where the proprietor is always on the edge of bankruptcy. Leaving this for his return to England, he runs completely out of funds; the job he had signed up for, as he says, "to take care of an idiot," had been postponed, and he has nothing to live on. Orwell therefore becomes a tramp, and walks across England from one "spike" to another ("spike" being a slang term for "poorhouse," where men who were not residents of the parish in which the poorhouses were located could spend only one might in each and then had to move on). He also spent time on the Embankment in London, where men and women who were literally homeless would spend the night attempting to sleep out of doors, as the Embankment-dwellers did not have the price of a bed. Finally, Orwell is rescued from this situation by a friend, and sets out to write about it.

This book contains some of the most graphic descriptions of poverty written in the twentieth century. One assumes that Orwell could have contacted school friends and acquaintances to obtain employment, even during a Depression. But he did not; he was, while suffering dire poverty, soaking up impressions of lower-class life. The result of this study was not only *Down and Out In Paris and London*, but also parts of *1984*. The account of the lives of the Proles, the description of the smelly close quarters in which most people are forced to live by the Party's deliberate edict - these were dividends from his years among the poor, and *1984* may profitably be read with this book as background. Orwell attempted to describe the life of the poor honestly, and because he went to such great lengths to study his subject, he succeeded to an unusual extent. The sympathies of most educated people, Orwell said, are not with the poor; they do not understand them. He at least attempted to understand, though he was not and never became a member of the submerged classes in terms of his outlook; his education and family background made this impossible.

Coming Up for Air (1939) is that novel of Orwell which most resembles *1984*. Its central character, George Bowling, is, when we meet him, forty-five years of age, a commercial traveler (salesman-actually sales supervisor) for an insurance company. He is intended by Orwell to be the epitome of the English lower middle class.

But George Bowling is, in a way, Winston Smith, in that he is the man who is just a little bit more perceptive and intelligent than is called for by his environment. George Bowling is a shopkeeper's son who is drafted into the British Army at the start of the First World War, and who becomes an officer and finds his life spared through several rather absurd coincidences. He has an opportunity to read, and he is naturally quick with his wits, so that he has in a sense moved somewhat apart from his class and environment and can therefore see these more clearly while remaining a part of them. The book is set in 1939, and Mr. Bowling is aware of the kind of world that is coming: "Fear! We swim in it. It's our element." This is a prediction of things to come; there is the sub-world of hatred and fear to which Bowling and all of his contemporaries are heading.

This novel, like *1984,* was more a warning than a prediction. This is the chronicle of the slightly ordinary extraordinary man in a society which is changing, probably for the worse, who is self-aware and who knows that things will never be the same. George Bowling is a fat man, in contrast to Winston Smith, who seems almost emaciated. But the two are one in their outlook on many things, especially in their pursuit of the Golden Country. Both George and Winston (note the heroic first names and the ordinary last names) are constantly seeking what they call the Golden Country. This appears to be a state before the Fall; a state of innocence into which they can retreat but which is an illusion. For Winston the Golden Country is the rural scene, akin to the Garden of Eden, in which he meets Julia. For George Bowling, when he returns to Lower Binfield, his home town, is also seeking this state of innocence. Thus, *Coming Up for Air* is also valuable background for a further understanding of *1984* in general and of Winston Smith in particular.

1984

ESSAY QUESTIONS AND ANSWERS

....

Question: Did Orwell write *1984* as a prediction of the state of world government and society in the year 1984?

Answer: *1984* was not intended to be a predication, and anyone reading it and deducing that Orwell meant it as such is mistaken; the evidence for this statement comes from the totality of Orwell's writing. It would be more accurate to say that Orwell was presenting the world of *1984* as a satiric statement of what might come to pass, though of course its exact form could never be predicted, if world society did not become aware of the terrible problems and contemporary tendencies facing it, not in 1984, but here and now-in the 1940s and early 1950s. Orwell wrote the book not as a prediction at all, but as a warning. For he believed that in many ways society was regressing back in the direction of barbarism, and that in the fight against fascism and other totalitarian and terroristic systems of government, even Western liberal society was being corrupted and was adopting the techniques used by its enemies.

In *Coming Up for Air* (1939), Orwell spelled out some of his fears: that hatred of fascism or communism would itself become a way of life and a profession; in other words, that decent men would in the end come to be defined by their enemies, so that instead of being for something, men in the Western democracies would end up by being against something, and that in turn this negative position would lead to totalitarianism.

The belief that *1984* was meant by Orwell to be a prediction of things to come probably rests on the evidence of the last third of the book, which seems exceptionally gloomy and pessimistic. But we know that Orwell was very ill at the time he wrote Part Three of *1984;* indeed, he died only a few months after *1984* was published. He was recorded as having remarked once that perhaps his illness had something to do with the dark outlook of Part Three. But as a man who was by nature an activist, fighting in Spain out of his ideological beliefs (which were changed somewhat by the experience), broadcasting during wartime for the B. B. C. after his health led to his rejection for military service, and writing essay after essay on vital political questions, Orwell sought to persuade and to change, not merely to record. And it is the evidence provided by his biography and his writings which leads to the conclusion that he wanted to reverse, by making them clear, the trends which he saw as culminating in the kind of society led by the Party and personified by Big Brother.

Question: What is the significance of Winston's dreams?

Answer: Winston is a man who is more self-aware and has more insight into his problems and his personality than most of the members of his society; this is part of the trouble and the reason for O'Brien's special interest in him. Winston is, by all decent standards, the sane man in the insane society. However, the Party's overwhelming strength-its machinery for thoughtcontrol-is such that O'Brien succeeds in breaking Winston and in convincing him that the Party represents the only sanity and that he, Winston, has been insane and is being cured by the Party. With these pressures on him, and with his limitations of intellect (for while he is intelligent, O'Brien is abstractly more intelligent), Winston of course does not have total insight into himself.

This is the function of his dreams: to show something of the psychological dynamics of his motivation in his revolt against the Party. He is cursed by feelings of guilt toward his mother and infant sister, and has recurring visions of them sinking out of sight in deep water. He has physical desire for the girl with the black hair in the Ministry of Truth, and this desire, repressed by the Party, finds expression in his dreams, as does his revolt against Party codes. Finally, in his dreams he discovers the Golden Country, which seems to be equated with existence as it had been in a happy, if perhaps nonexistent, past. Guilt feelings, repressed sexuality, and euphoria: these emotions, according to Freudian theory, when repressed, spill over from the unconscious and can provide an outside observer with clues to motivation and to the unconscious interests and desires of the dreamer. Winston Smith's dreams should be treated by the reader as being of considerable importance in the effort to understand him.

Question: Why is the headquarters of the Thought Police and the repressive apparatus of the Party called "The Ministry of Love?"

Answer: In a paradoxical way, as both Goldstein's Book, *The Theory and Practice of Oligarchical Collectivism*, and O'Brien tell Winston Smith, the Party must save its members who go astray from themselves, while at the same time demonstrating its limitless power to crush the individual. But O'Brien "loves" Winston Smith, not necessarily in a perverted way, but because he desires to make him perfect, as he tells Winston during one of the torture sessions. He regards Winston as a sick man, in fact a lunatic, who must be made whole, and torture is the instrument by which Winston's salvation will be accomplished. Not only should Winston love the embodiment of the Party, Big Brother, as he does at the end, but Big Brother loves him. It is the function of the torture in the Ministry of Love to make Winston perfect, within the terms of his insane society, even if that society demands of him that he must believe that two plus two make five.

O'Brien and the Party have watched over Winston for seven years, and this is one more sign that Big Brother "loves" Winston. He, Winston, is, as O'Brien tells him, "a flaw in the pattern which must be wiped out." This does not even necessarily import his physical death, but the death of his spirit through the killing of the one human relationship he had ever experienced as an adult: the relationship with Julia. Winston is a very minor figure, but in terms of what he represents to the Party he is worth endless effort and trouble, and in fact is worth the extremely complicated steps the Party takes to entrap him and exercise its power over him. Therefore, the Ministry, though it seems to be constructed on sheer hatred, is transposed into the Ministry of Love, as symbol of the satiric treatment which Orwell accords to the "love" with which the Party regards even its humblest servants when they go astray and fall into Thoughtcrime.

Question: What is the relation of James Burnham's work to *1984*?

Answer: Burnham, a political theorist, wrote in 1941 *The Managerial Revolution* as a sort of prediction of things to come; he envisioned a society which would be rigidly hierarchical, with a small aristocracy of talent at the top and a large class of semi-slaves at the bottom. Orwell was concerned to refute

Burnham, and did so in a pamphlet published in 1946, *Second Thoughts on James Burnham*, which called into question the accuracy of Burnham's predictions, and which seems to have provided much of the intellectual background for the structure of Oceanic society in *1984.*

Question: Why does Orwell represent the society of *1984* as being in a state of perpetual war, yet with no decisive victory?

Answer: The answer is to be found in Goldstein's book, *The Theory and Practice of Oligarchical Collectivism*, in which it is observed that war provides a psychologically acceptable means of destroying any surplus goods which might make life more comfortable and therefore lead people to be less fanatical and hysterical through deprivation. "War is Peace," because in a state of constant, or chronic war, a certain stability is assured. The ruling classes of each of the three great superstates have decided that war can only go so far-without admitting these things to themselves-or else everything will be destroyed. War, then, can exist as an instrument for stabilizing and unifying a society internally, but without any real purpose of "victory." One could, in fact, coin a Party phrase which might be applied to war as it is waged in *1984:* "Victory is defeat!"

Question: Contrast the form of the revolt against Big Brother of Julia and Winston Smith.

Answer: Julia's revolt is only on the physical level, while Winston's is on the more fundamental intellectual level, which makes him, in the Party's eyes, a much more dangerous criminal than Julia. Of course, Winston has no chance of succeeding in what he tries to accomplish, because the Party has been watching him from the beginning, long before he was even conscious of his total dissatisfaction with the system under which his society lives and works. Julia does not consider ideology at all, and falls asleep when Winston reads to her from Goldstein's book. She hates the system, but cannot see that Goldstein's book at least explains it. This is because Julia is incapable of holding an ideology; she rejects all abstractions, and rebels physically. But, when she is arrested with Winston, her physical strength is weak in comparison to the limitless force which the Party can use against her. So Julia confesses quickly, whereas Winston puts up a fight which is inspiring, even though we know that he must lose.

Question: What is the relation of *Down and Out in Paris and London* and *Coming Up for Air* to *1984*?

Answer: The first book (1933) is a study of severe poverty and of its degrading effects on the human being. Orwell shows the Party in *1984* consciously using all forms of physical deprivation to control its citizens. Further, he tries to describe the life of the Proles, about which "little is known." What he learned of lower-class life he learned at firsthand, and this is chronicled in the earlier *Down and Out in Paris and London*.

Coming Up for Air contrasts two symbols which Orwell uses at length in *1984:* the Golden Country and the subworld of totalitarianism. George Bowling, the hero of *Coming Up for Air*, can see the kind of world which is in store for him and his generation. It is a world of "coloured shirts, machine-guns, barbed wire, concentration camps, etc." On the other hand he remembers back to his boyhood days in Lower Binfield, which are all symbolized for him by a dark pool where there were some of the largest and most tempting fish in the area. The pool and its surroundings, unspoiled and undiscovered as they are, are part of the Golden Country, the state of innocence, perhaps the Garden of Eden, for George Bowling. This motif of the Golden Country also runs through Winston Smith's thoughts and dreams.

Question: What is the meaning of Orwell's choice of the name Winston Smith for his hero?

Answer: Smith is the most common English name, and tends to establish our hero as Everyman in his society. He undergoes a universal experience. At the same time, Winston is the name of the great twentieth-century Prime Minister, Sir Winston Churchill, who was a most uncommon man, and quite probably the greatest Englishman of his age. And so is Winston Smith an uncommon man. Simply refusing to accept his warped society as it is; believing as he does that sanity is not statistical but objective, Winston Smith is a most uncommon man. The two concepts of him, then, are maintained by the author simultaneously: common, or representative man, and unusual and sensitive man. Both coexist in Winston Smith's personality, and both are symbolized by his name.

Question: What is the function of the Proles in the society of *1984?*

Answer: The Proles are ignored by the Party, except for the very rare threat which an individual Prole of ability might pose. Proles are not allowed to rise into the Inner or Outer Party; one who might become dangerous is simply marked down and eliminated by the agents of the Thought Police who move concealed among the Proles. "Proles and animals are free" is the Party slogan. But "free" has a special meaning; it means, within the context of *1984,* beneath contempt: too low to merit the discipline of the Party. Yet some 85% of the population are Proles, and according to the Party's political mythology, the Revolution (i.e. the revolution which brought the principles of

Ingsoc, the Party, and Big Brother to power) was made for the Proles, or workers.

As Emmanuel Goldstein's Book explains, society, since the dawn of human history, has been divided into the Low, the Middle, and the High. Since the High (the Inner Party) in *1984* is for the first time a ruling class which is completely self-conscious about its desire for power, the usual change in which the Middle changes place with the High with the co-operation and aid of the Low cannot occur. A moment in history is frozen forever by the High. Winston Smith perceives this, and also perceives that since the members of the Inner and Outer Parties are, as he says to Julia, no longer human, such hope as there is for the future lies in the Proles-if they can only become self-aware. But, as O'Brien tells Winston, this is not likely to happen.

Question: Is *1984* a **satire** on Communism?

Answer: The answer to this lies in an interpretation of all available evidence from Orwell's life and work. Orwell said that since 1936 all of his efforts, whether exerted in his primary area of talent - the writing of fiction, essays, and other forms of written expression, or exerted in other directions, such as his service in the Spanish Civil War and in the Home Guard in England during the Second World War - had been in pursuit of his fight against totalitarianism. Orwell consciously sets himself against every form of tyranny over the mind and heart and body of man. Thus he was against all forms of totalitarianism, of which Communism, and especially the Stalinist variety which he saw only too vividly in action in Spain, is but one form.

It is more correct to say, therefore, that *1984* satirizes all absolutist systems of political control of man, whether they are called Communism, Fascism, or a number of other varieties -

what might be called Managerialism (in James Burnham's sense, which Orwell attacked), or Oligarchical Collectivism, which is the form of government of *1984,* whatever else the Party may call it. What these forms have in common is that none is democratic in any commonly - received sense of the word. Orwell was essentially a democratic Socialist in political outlook - probably with a Swiftian admixture of skepticism concerning man's potentiality for degrading himself and doing evil. He did not believe that man's nature could sustain the gift of supreme power and in matters of power was more a rationalist and a believer in checks and balances, which are present by their absence in *1984.*

It should be kept in mind, in answering this question, that O'Brien himself presents the Inner Party to Winston Smith as the "successors" of the Communists and other totalitarians of the first half of the twentieth century. This brings us back to a cardinal point about the **satire** of *1984:* that the book was a satiric projection of trends which Orwell saw in his own age, in the decades of the 1930s and 1940s. Only one of these trends was Communism.

Question: What is the function of technology in *1984?*

Answer: While our age is a technological age, Orwell saw that the machine and the ingenious technology of this century could be made to achieve totally corrupt ends. By 1984, in his satirical picture of society, the men who matter are interested only in power over people; power over things is secondary. Science, which by nature and methodology calls for the strictest objectivity, is against the spirit of the totalitarian state of Oceania, and disinterested basic scientific research for the sake of gaining knowledge, which might or might not be "practical," has disappeared. Just as art and literature, the most enduring records of the greatness of certain civilizations, have been perverted in *1984,* so science has been perverted, and the practical result of science: technology.

Insofar as there is any scientific research still being conducted in Oceania, it is directed toward an even deeper enslavement of the population, if that is possible. Two vast problems are being studied; how to kill several hundred million people in a few seconds with no possibility of advance warning, and how to find out what a person is thinking against his will. Orwell makes the grim suggestion that the Party is making progress in both areas, though by 1984 it has not actually succeeded. Probably the first objective is one which the Party does not really wish to attain, though by the principles of Doublethink it appears to want such absolute weapons as instruments of victory over Eurasia and Eastasia with consequent world domination. The second objective is more likely to be attained, because the Party cannot stand that even one individual, such as Winston Smith, can have a heterodox thought. When and if the Party can make such progress that it can actually read a man's thoughts, there will be total tyranny, and science, or what is left of science- certainly not the spirit of scientific inquiry as we know it today- will have become corruptive rather than a force liberating man and increasing his control of his environment and his power for good. Thus it is better to describe such inquiry and investigation as still exists in *1984* as technology and not science, because what the Party is engaged in is not really scientific inquiry at all.

www.ingramcontent.com/pod-product-compliance
Lightning Source LLC
LaVergne TN
LVHW011716060526
838200LV00051B/2911